you can find inspiration in everything*

paul smith

*and if you can't, look again

Thames & Hudson

in association with Violette Editions

for pauline, my love and my inspiration – p. s.

First Published in Great Britain in 2001 by Violette Editions, an imprint of Violette Limited
First Published in paperback in Great Britain in 2003 by Thames & Hudson Ltd, 181A High Holborn,
London WC1V 7QX, in association with Violette Editions

Edited and produced by Robert Violette
Art direction by Alan Aboud and design by Alan Aboud, Emma Jones, Ellie Ridsdale, Mark Thomson,
Zoë Symonds and Maxine Law at Aboud•Sodano, London
Copy editing and proofreading by Vanessa Mitchell and Irena Hoare • picture research by Jo Walton
Additional research and assistance by Susanna Scouller • production assistance by Kyoko Tachibana

For their invaluable assistance with this project, Violette Editions wishes to thank: Jonathan Towle, Håkan
Rosenius, Liz Hasell, Ken Okada, Colette Youell, Louise Thompson, Graham Addinall, Derek Morton, Nicola
Smaridge, Sandra Hill, Boo Hodges, Lance Martins, Sophie Boilley, Michiko Katsura, Kumi Ota, Gary Ota,
Kumi Kudera, Teresa Ramsden, Debbie Waite, Cindy Vieira, Sabrina Bosenberg, Ashley Long, John Morley,
Boris Uran, Helena Marn, Jonathan Ive, Carter Multz, Michael Cooke, John Thornberry, Brian Neeson,
Bridget Bouch, Mari Katainen, Jasmine Chung, Martha Millard, Keith Gray, Mick Hodgson, Glen Baxter,
Mick Brownfied, Paul Slater, Alan Fletcher, Michael Macdonald-Cooper, Katsu, Family Inner Ocean, Kacchi,
James Cant, George Baptista, Izumi Hiroshima, Kerstin Gleba, Moko Tanaka, Alessandra Merchetti,
Elizabeth Beyer, Damian Jones, Melanie Mues, Octavia Wiseman and Sandy Violette

Select copyright-free images used in this publication were sourced from a series of books published
by Dover Publications, Inc.

Statements by Paul Smith in this publication are drawn from conversations with the editor or are selected
and edited, with Paul Smith, from texts by, articles about or interviews with Paul Smith published between
1970 and 2001 in the following publications: *Arena, The Bristol Evening Post, Capital Magazine, Covent
Garden Courier, The Daily Express, The Daily Telegraph, Design Week, Drapers Record, Elle, Esquire,
ES Magazine, The Face, FHM, FHM Collections, The Financial Times, GQ, The Guardian, The Guardian
Weekend Magazine, Harpers & Queen, i-D, The Independent Magazine, The Independent on Sunday,
Later, Live IT, MAB News, The Mail on Sunday, Man Magazine, Nottingham Evening Post, The Observer
Life Magazine, Sunday Morning Post Magazine, The Sunday Times, Sunday Today, The Telegraph
Weekend Magazine, Themepark, The Times, True Brit* (exhibition catalogue, The Design Museum, 1985),
Vogue and *Where*

Portrait of Paul Smith on page 8 by Sandro Sodano

A CIP record for this book is available from the British Library
ISBN 0-500-28445-8

Printed and bound in Slovenia by Mladinska Knjiga Tiskarna

contents

reader:

go forwards,
don't go backwards,
and remember,
many a true string
said in vest.

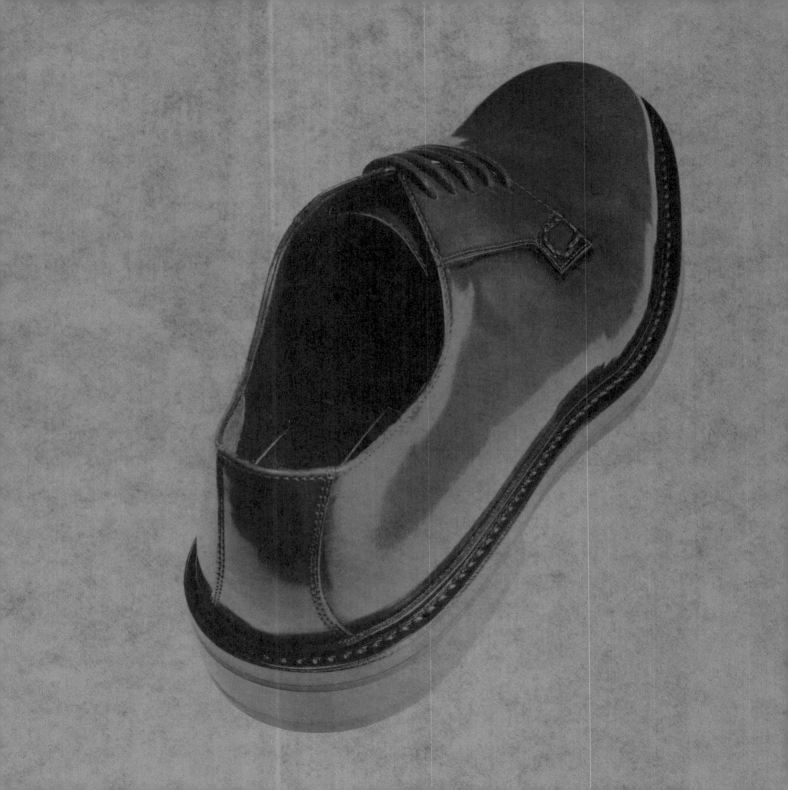

esattamente ciò che indossava Steve McQueen nella Grande fuga, ed ecco perché il sito web della Polo offre "classici" usati d'annata a prezzi svariate volte superiori rispetto alle riproduzioni, spesso meticolose, che Mr Lauren fa oggi di quegli stessi articoli.

I modelli di Paul Smith sembrano provenire da una straordinaria ed enciclopedica consapevolezza della natura, potentemente codificata, della "britannicità". È come se avesse un equivalente interno dello Houndsditch Clothes Exchange, non un museo ma una vasta, infinita, combinatoria vendita di beneficenza, nella quale tutti i manufatti e tutta la cultura della sua nazione si impegnano in un costante scambio reciproco di codici. Possedere un articolo di Paul Smith significa così possedere qualcosa (molto) di più della somma totale dei codici incarnati in quell'articolo. È una sorta di poesia al lavoro, l'equivalente della consapevolezza letteraria del peso del mondo assente. È allo stesso tempo sottile e molto robusta, questa qualità, e a essa attribuisco il fatto che molti dei miei capi d'abbigliamento preferiti, negli ultimi vent'anni, sono stati disegnati da Paul Smith.

Un paio di scarpe pesanti di pelle zigrinata, marrone medio, convertite in qualcosa di totalmente diverso dalle suole scelte dallo stilista: le stesse suole nere a carro armato preferite dagli skinhead che non vogliono affidare l'intensità del loro fastidio alle più tenere cure delle Dr. Martens. Assolutamente perfette. Di conseguenza, le uniche scarpe che possano reggere il confronto: le Storm Derby originali di Oliver Sweeney, una scarpa che ho sempre pensato avrebbe potuto essere stata disegnata da Paul Smith.

Una camicia molto seria e molto formale, polsini doppi, collo classico, confezionata con il più scuro dei denim indaco. È stata forse la camicia più d'effetto che abbia mai avuto, capace di allontanare l'attenzione da qualunque vestito e di conferire a chi la porta un grado stranamente ammissibile di eleganza cowboy-piratesca, anche in situazioni in cui, di norma, l'eleganza cowboy-piratesca non sarebbe permessa.

Una cintura di cuoio marrone, perfettamente semplice e liscia, metà anni Novanta, che incarna e tuttavia in qualche modo supera tutto quanto di grande c'era nella ricontestualizzazione americana che ho descritto prima. Senza cuciture, un'unica lista di cuoio da finimenti incredibilmente spesso e flessibile, con una pesante fibbia a rullo fissata a un'estremità. È la cintura che gli hippie produttori di sandali a Haight-Ashbury e all'East Village si sforzavano di fare senza probabilmente esserci mai riusciti. È l'idea platonica di una cintura di cuoio marrone da indossare con i jeans.

La "P.C.," una camicia della prima collezione della linea R. Newbold. La camicia dei poliziotti inglesi, identica a quella di poliestere che si trova nei negozi Oxfam, ma resa con un sottile cotone grezzo che ricorda le uniformi indiane del Raj. Completa di ogni dettaglio, fino alle doppie asole per ancorare le spalline, ma deviata su un binario cronologico alternativo dal tessuto e dalla scelta dei bottoni (grossi pezzi di plastica liscia, senza tratti caratteristici, simili a quelli che usavano i sarti per agganciare comodamente le bretelle). Tagliata molto ampia, con una doppia cucitura anteriore, stretta in vita per aprirsi in fondo, è brillantemente trasandata se portata con i lembi fuori, e tuttavia vagamente minacciosa e orwelliana se indossata dentro i calzoni.

Pantaloni "P.T.," sempre della linea R. Newbold. Ampi, capaci, assurdamente comodi, fanno sembrare formali e ricercati i soliti calzoni da lavoro con molte tasche. Drill di cotone, conciato con una sfumatura fumosa e decisamente poco militare di un soffocato rosso borgogna. Un altro paio di calzoni – interni (una fodera integrale e staccata), fatti di cotone da fazzoletto – offre un calore stupefacente nei climi freddi.

Una cravatta, di uno spento fustagno canna di fucile, ornata da un transfer fotografico di dieci centimetri quadrati con mucche su un prato, e dietro di esse, contro l'orizzonte, il grande radiotelescopio di Jodrell Bank.

Un pullover molto lungo, molto verde, molto meraviglioso, molto compianto, che è stato in realtà il mio primo vero acquisto in Floral Street. Ci andai il giorno dopo una tempesta di neve, alla fine degli anni Ottanta, attonito davanti alla rivelazione di una Londra che non avevo mai visto prima. Una Londra silenziosa e più misteriosa del solito, sotto un tessuto di neve sudicia, ma capace di trasformarla in maniera radicale.

Ai miei occhi, l'Inghilterra e il Giappone sono le due nazioni "più profonde", le più inesauribilmente e perfettamente affascinanti. Le loro rispettive culture sono codificate in un modo così peculiare, significato entro significato, fino a una struttura frattale a quanto pare invisibile a gran parte degli indigeni dei due paesi. Nazioni insulari, universi tascabili, psicogeografie di immani durate mai interrotte, sono sedi di passati imperi e poli di industrializzazione nelle rispettive arene geopolitiche. (I giapponesi hanno comprato dagli inglesi il kit completo per la rivoluzione industriale. Se ne sono deliberatamente infettati. Hanno perso la testa. Sono crollati. Ne sono emersi come la prima nazione industriale dell'Asia.)

Londra e Tokyo possiedono un'irriflessa fiducia in se stesse. Parigi è in perpetuo, e in modo narcisistico, consapevole di sé, e New York ha sempre bisogno di ricevere complimenti. Gli abitanti di Londra e di Tokyo sono ammiratori consumati di "marchi segreti"; mettono in scena drammi privati attorno al loro status di consumatori con una gravitas di rado vista altrove. Sia gli inglesi sia i giapponesi sono abilissimi importatori. Se volete sapere che cosa produce di veramente eccellente la vostra nazione, guardate cosa hanno scelto di importare i più acuti (ossessivamente acuti) dei residenti di Londra e Tokyo. Osservate le scelte degli otaku, i fanatici della pura informazione.

La mia casa editrice, agli inizi della mia carriera di romanziere, era la Victor Gollancz, i cui uffici erano in Henrietta Street. Arrivai a conoscere bene Covent Garden. Un "giro pubblicitario" inglese, in quell'epoca, consisteva in gran parte nel fermarsi a Covent Garden, aspettando i giornalisti e i fotografi che avevano accettato di farsi vedere. Se non avevo appuntamenti per l'ora seguente, potevo ampliare un po' i miei orizzonti. E fu così che scoprii Paul Smith nello scenario del suo negozio. Dopo aver vagabondato in quella che credevo fosse la direzione approssimativa di Seven Dials, sbagliai strada, senza avere in realtà lasciato Covent Garden, e mi ritrovai in Floral Street.

Allora non c'era un distributore ufficiale di Paul Smith in Canada (e non sono sicuro che ci sia nemmeno oggi). Quel poco di Paul Smith che riusciva a raggiungere i negozi canadesi tendeva a essere costoso in maniera surreale, e qualunque negoziante che lo aveva in vetrina sembrava più deciso a farne un punto d'onore che a venderlo. E spesso, come succede, non si vendeva, non a quei prezzi, ed era semmai avvicinabile in gennaio, se si aveva molta fortuna, a prezzi simili a quelli pieni delle importazioni dall'Italia. Così mi ero procurato alcuni articoli di Paul Smith, di cui conoscevo il nome per averlo letto nelle riviste di moda inglesi; soprattutto camicie, e mi erano piaciute molto.

Faceva questa piccolissima cosa, meravigliosamente perversa, con i polsini. Fino a quel momento, per me, i polsini erano sempre stati normali polsini, ma con un'asola in più dalla parte del bottone, così da permettere l'uso di gemelli.

Il gemelli, a quell'epoca, erano nell'America del Nord virtualmente estinti: erano inutili come i bottoncini per fissare il collo alla camicia. E mi era stato insegnato, attraverso il codice americano della mia giovinezza, che i cosiddetti polsini "convertibili" erano in sé degradati, e molto probabilmente erano il tratto distintivo di un indumento di qualità inferiore. Ma Paul Smith li impiegava. Sembravano essere una sorta di segreto marchio di fabbrica, e lui li ha sempre fatti, a meno che i polsini non fossero doppi. Li faceva a prescindere dal tessuto o dalla relativa informalità di una particolare camicia, e pertanto offriva sempre questa stravagante e nascosta opzione di stile.

Non posso dire con assoluta sicurezza che quella visita, in mezzo alla neve ridotta a fanghiglia, fosse la mia prima esperienza del negozio di Floral Street, e anzi sospetto che non lo fosse. Ma fu la prima volta che lo capii davvero. Forse, in precedenza, ero ancora sotto l'effetto del cambio di fuso orario, e quasi di sicuro ero intimidito da quelli che mi parevano i segni della ricchezza e della moda, due qualità che non possedevo.

Ma quel giorno, arrivandoci per caso, mi apparve (e in realtà lo è) un prodigio estremamente benevolo.

Mi fece venire in mente alcuni negozi molto contegnosi e immensamente démodé di Barcellona e Roma, alla fine degli anni Sessanta. Posti così vittoriani che non prevedevano nemmeno l'esposizione delle merci. Dove, se chiedevate dei calzini, qualcuno andava a prenderveli a una parete di cassettiere di quercia numerate. Poiché il negozio di Floral Street è un collage di accessori vittoriani, e benché gli articoli siano senza dubbio esposti, appartiene in qualche modo allo stesso contesto delle cassettiere numerate. Sembrava uno dei negozi più attraenti che avessi mai visto, e lo è ancora.

E, quasi per mettere fine a qualunque esitazione che mi potesse frenare, erano in corso i saldi di gennaio. La gente si accalcava scompigliando le camicie piegate e palpando tavoli di cravatte, ed ebbi la sensazione di poter fare lo stesso senza rischi. E lo feci.

Emergendo alla fine, dopo aver percorso da cima a fondo l'intero negozio, con questo meraviglioso pullover verde, di un cotone molto pesante, lavorato a cordoncino, nella più bella e vibrante sfumatura di verde scuro. Per molto tempo, non me lo tolsi quasi di dosso. E poi passò a mia moglie, e divenne uno dei suoi capi preferiti, e lo portò per vari anni ancora, quando lavorava in giardino, finché, immagino, cadde a brandelli, letteralmente.

Paul Smith shop, Floral Street, Covent Garden, London (photos: Mat Buck).

Amo lo stile e non sempre mi piace la moda, e la mia idea di un grande stilista, e in particolare di uno stilista di abbigliamento maschile, si riduce di fatto a una persona capace di produrre indumenti molto speciali, molto memorabili, che diventano, proprio come quel maglione verde, i nostri capi preferiti. Articoli che non vengono mai abbandonati, una volta acquistati, ma che restano a portata di mano finché non cadono a pezzi. Quanto è rara, una cosa del genere.

Paul Smith, direi, ha fatto e fa sempre così. I suoi modelli sono personali in un modo che di solito non associamo a stilisti di madrelingua inglese (e se accade, tendono a essere quasi invariabilmente britannici). Ma ciò che, per me, ha sempre distinto Paul Smith dagli altri stilisti, anche dagli altri stilisti inglesi, è quel senso di un interno Houndsditch Clothes Exchange. Quella ricombinatoria Biblioteca di Babele sartoriale, nella quale tutti i testi rifluiscono in tutti gli altri testi, e il "nuovo" arriva direttamente e in perfetto orario dagli intricati e interdipendenti ammassi di codici che generano (e sottostanno a) ciò che è, dopo tutto, una cultura estremamente antica e intricata. Nella quale il "nuovo" arriva in un contesto.

Questo non implica, fra parentesi, che Paul Smith sia semplicemente il creatore di un brevettato stile classico con eccentricità incorporata, di cose robuste e piuttosto costose che uno conserva per anni. È anche questo, naturalmente, ma c'è sempre qualche altro fattore in campo, e in effetti lui disegna cose che apprezzo in astratto ma non avrei un particolare desiderio di indossare. Non mi sento a mio agio a indossare abiti esasperati, e Paul Smith, in alcuni dei suoi modelli, continua a manifestare una specie di geniale ferocia alla Duchamp. (I surrealisti erano ben noti, ai loro tempi, quasi senza eccezioni, per essere dei veri dandy.)

Ritengo che questo lato di Paul Smith sia l'esito di un deliberato ampliamento di lunghezza d'onda, fino a comprendere codici "stranieri". Non solo codici di abiti, ma codici dell'intero universo umano dei manufatti. Voi o io, in India, possiamo notare un ripiano di bancone in un logoro laminato blu. Credo che Paul Smith, guardando quello stesso bancone, possa vederci una camicia, o il tessuto con cui dovrebbe essere fatta una camicia.

Chiavi visibili per penetrare in questo aspetto del suo processo creativo sono forse quei singolari prodotti e manufatti, scoperti da Paul Smith nel corso dei suoi viaggi, che i visitatori, talvolta incuriositi e confusi, trovano nei suoi negozi. Cose bizzarre e comunissime (in qualche contesto originale che uno potrebbe immaginare) e meravigliose, rivelate dall'occhio dello stilista e a loro volta rivelatrici.

Ho il sospetto, sulla base degli oggetti giapponesi incontrati nei suoi negozi, che un album di istantanee di Tokyo scattate da Paul Smith rivelerebbe l'essenza di Tokyo che anch'io ho potuto scorgere ma che non sono mai riuscito a fotografare. In realtà, la sua idea di Tokyo ha modellato la mia prima ancora che ci andassi, e quando ci andai davvero, vidi all'istante ciò che aveva colto lui.

E a Tokyo, mi informò la guida nel corso della mia prima visita, era stata allestita, in onore del grande Paul Smith, una mostra dei suoi disegni, e anche di quelli che venivano considerati oggetti rari e che incarnavano la quintessenza di ciò che è inglese. E il più popolare fra essi, mi informò il traduttore, era stata una di quelle straordinarie auto sportive, le Mini Cooper, quelle con tre sole ruote. Una volta ne avevo intravista una in autostrada, uno strano sogno con cinghie di cuoio per fissare il cofano, come una macchina uscita da un romanzo di Michael Moorcock. Imparai in quella circostanza, anche se da allora l'ho dimenticata, la parola giapponese che significa "desiderio di essere ciò che per natura non si può essere".

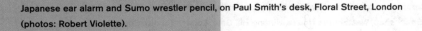

Japanese ear alarm and Sumo wrestler pencil, on Paul Smith's desk, Floral Street, London (photos: Robert Violette).

Mi fu insegnata, immagino, mentre mi veniva spiegato il fascino che Paul Smith esercita sui giapponesi, e il fascino di quella Mini folle e meravigliosa.

Ma io non ho mai desiderato essere inglese, e non credo che nemmeno gli appassionati giapponesi di Paul Smith vogliano essere inglesi. Per me, e credo anche per loro, è una questione di codici. Il suo Houndsditch Exchange. La sua padronanza dei codici più profondi, nella quale con tutta probabilità è senza eguali.

Sono passati vari anni da quando ho scoperto per la prima volta quelle camicie con l'asola segreta in più, e Paul Smith rimane per me lo stilista più interessante. Perché continua ad articolare qualcosa, qualcosa di tanto complesso come un'intera cultura, nel codice – limitato eppure infinitamente ricombinabile – di fibra e tessuto e colore e taglio.

L'anno scorso, mentre vagabondavo, stordito dal cambio di fuso, dal mio hotel di Notting Hill verso Portobello, nell'oscurità che precede l'alba estiva, mi sono imbattuto per la prima volta nel negozio di Paul Smith in Westbourne Grove. Fluttuava all'angolo, con le vetrine meravigliosamente illuminate in mezzo al tessuto di quel mistero involuto e inesplicabile che è Londra. Perfetto, una volta di più, e situato perfettamente sul reticolo di quel mistero, appena fuori Portobello Market, dove i codici di innumerevoli oggetti costruiti dall'uomo comunicano in una gloriosa complessità, in quell'ora, nell'oscurità di chiuse scatole di vetro in cento gallerie improvvisate.

Mini Cooper car customised by Paul Smith (photo: Sandro Sodano).
Paul Smith shop, Westbourne House, Notting Hill Gate, London (photo: Sonia Peric).

paul smith: ein wunder im besten sinne   william gibson

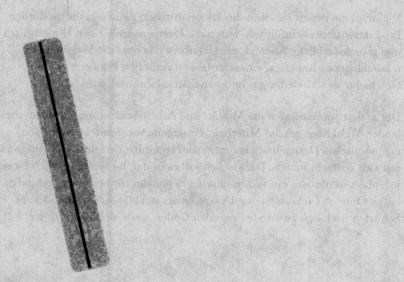

Vor hundertfünfzig Jahren lag an der Südgrenze der Londoner City, in der Nähe des südlichen Endes der Petticoat Lane, ein ungefähr einen Morgen großes, rechteckiges, ödes und feuchtes Gelände mit einem Bretterzaun drum herum. Das war die Houndsditch Clothes Exchange, wo Händler vor schmutzigen Haufen von Stiefeln, Kleidern, Schirmen, Peitschen und allerlei anderen gebrauchten und ausrangierten Gegenständen auf Bänken hockten. Hier wurden gestohlene Kleidungsstücke „umgearbeitet" (man entfernte ihre Etiketten und alle Kennzeichnungen), und getragene Kleidung von besserer Qualität wurde an Händler in kleinen Nebenstraßen weiterverhökert, die vielleicht ein Wams aus den Resten von zweien zusammenflickten oder nicht lange vorhaltende Wunder an kaputten Stiefeln wirkten. Diese zwielichtige und für unsere Augen überaus Dickenssche Einrichtung hatte, im Nachhinein betrachtet, mehr mit der Zukunft der britischen Herrenbekleidung zu tun als sämtliche Aktivitäten der Schneider, die zur damaligen Zeit en vogue waren. Die Umarbeiter, die in Houndsditch kauften, taten unwissentlich etwas sehr Modernes: Sie rekombinierten die Codes von Schnitt und Stoff und schufen dadurch Kleidungsstücke, die es zuvor nicht gegeben hatte.

Während die neuen Fabriken des viktorianischen Zeitalters die modernen Produktionsmittel einführten, waren die Lumpenhändler von Houndsditch und ihre gewerbliche Klientel, die Umarbeiter, bereits die Vorboten des rekombinanten Impulses, eines der beiden zentralen Faktoren in der Geschichte des Modedesigns im zwanzigsten Jahrhundert.

Der andere war natürlich die Militär- und Arbeitsbekleidung, nachdem die beiden Weltkriege präzise Mittel zur Festlegung von Konfektionsgrößen, ergonomisches Design und eine rationale, scheinbar designfreie Nichtästhetik mit sich gebracht hatten. Dazwischen gab es in der Tat wenig wirklich Neues; jedenfalls wenig, was ein viktorianischer Schneider für besonders gefunden hätte. Ohne das rekombinante Design, unser unablässiges postmodernes Schürfen nach den zugrunde liegenden Codes, sowie den Einfluss der

'The Houndsditch Macaroni', 1772, J. Bretherton (photo: Guildhall Library, Corporation of London).

Arbeitsbekleidung und der Armeerest-restbestände abzieht, bleibt nur noch ein müdes Simulacrum der traditionellen britischen Herrenschneiderei.

Oder sagen wir, man hat den Zustand der britischen Herrenmode am Ende des letzten Krieges, kurz vor dem Auftauchen neuer Paradigmen. Man hat den „demob suit", den man bei der Entlassung vom Militär bekam, und ein paar randständige Bohemiens des New-Edwardian-Style, dessen Codes jedoch allmählich schon ins Erbe der Teds übergingen. In Amerika wurde den Männern währenddessen dank Brooks Brothers und ihrer zahllosen Nachahmer ein ironiefreies Phantasma des Pseudo-Englischen verkauft.

Moss Brothers und Brooks Brothers, und dazwischen der graue Atlantik.

Meine amerikanische Kindheit war reich gesegnet mit Button-down-Hemden (ursprünglich eine von britischen Polospielern übernommene unkonventionelle Kragen-Modifikation) und Accessoires in Regimentalstreifen. Ein humorloser Mischmasch geborgter Codes, zusammengebaut im Dienst einer sonderbar unechten Nostalgie, die aus New England kam (obwohl sie auch im Süden, wo ich aufgewachsen bin, enorm stark und populär war und es auch heute noch ist).

Die Ivy League war das Einzige, was es gab, zumindest im „besseren" Milieu. In genau dieses amerikanische Eden vor dem Sündenfall führte Ralph Lauren eine sehr lange Dekade später die von den Sixties aufgeriebenen Überreste meiner Generation von Amerikanern zurück und verdiente sich dabei eine goldene Nase.

Doch Mitte der sechziger Jahre tat sich etwas in England, in einem winzigen, überaus elitären Zirkel von Soho-Style-Otakus – etwas, was den Ivy-League-Code wieder in die Nation zurückholte, die seine Eltern-Memmen hervorgebracht hatte. In einer Serie phantasievoller Wiederaneignungen durch diese modernistischen Fanatiker, diese Ur-Mods, wurde das amerikanische Button-down-Hemd zusammen mit Khaki-Hosen, Gold-Cup-Sportsocken und Bass-Weejuns-Slippern geradezu heimlich importiert und in einen völlig neuen Kontext gestellt. In den Händen dieser detailverliebten, scharfäugigen

Teddy boys, 1950s (photo: Hulton Archive).
British soldiers, 1915 (photo: Mary Evans Picture Library).

Besessenen wurden Americana-Elemente mit bewusster anglophiler Tendenz auf eine kulturelle Mission geschickt, die meine Schulkameraden und ich niemals begriffen hätten. Im London der Mitte der sechziger Jahre bedeuteten diese Kleidungsstücke etwas anderes, etwas ganz Neues und Großartiges. Sie wurden die zentrale Geste einer einzigartigen Form von Unabhängigkeit, die Wurzeln eines Impulses, von dem meine amerikanischen Freunde und ich eigentlich erst etwas mitbekommen konnten, als wir Michael Caine's minimalistische Cockney-Coolness in „Ipcress" bewundern konnten.

Wir waren gerade dabei, diese Stile, die in ihrem ursprünglichen Kontext eine so andere Bedeutung hatten, hinter uns zu lassen. Wir entdeckten die Schönheiten des Army-Navy-Stores, wo man grandiose und grandios billige Chambray-Arbeitshemden, klassische Levi's, lederne Dienstgürtel mit eckiger Schnalle und vieles mehr finden konnte. Bei der Morgenröte dieser amerikanischen Rekontextualisierung stand das Neue, die Entdeckung im Vordergrund. Tom Wolfes Ansicht, wir hätten uns nur auf mitleiderregende Weise die Potenz der Arbeiterklasse ausborgen wollen, habe ich nie geteilt. Ich bezweifle, dass Tom Wolfe jemals ein paar Levi's besessen hat, selbst als Levi's noch Levi's waren. Und heute gehören den Japanern die originalen Webstühle, mit denen der Denim der Levi's, an die ich mich erinnere, hergestellt wurde, und wenn ich wieder so eine Hose haben will, muss ich mir entweder französische oder holländische Jeans kaufen, die in Tunesien aus exklusiv in Japan gewebtem Stoff zusammengenäht worden sind.

Sie hat nicht sehr lange gedauert, diese erste Phase der Rekontextualisierung in Amerika. Sie sollte bald in einem überkandidelten Meer aus Fransen und Kristallen untergehen, und zu einem gewissem Grad in den Produkten der Carnaby Street, eines kurzlebigen Impulses, der in nicht unerheblichem Ausmaß in jener ursprünglichen britischen Rekontextualisierung wurzelte. Doch diese beiden kurzen stilistischen Perioden auf beiden Seiten des Atlantiks haben die Mode in aller Welt fortan tiefgreifend beeinflusst. Deshalb sieht man junge Männer in Tokio, die auch heute noch sehr viel Sorgfalt darauf

Michael Caine, 'The Ipcress File' (photo: Lowndes Productions, The Kobal Collection).

verwenden, sich genauso zu kleiden wie Steve McQueen in „Gesprengte Ketten", und deshalb bietet die Polo-Website museumsreife Second-Hand-„Classics" zum vielfachen Preis von Mr. Laurens oftmals überaus exakten Reproduktionen derselben Kleidungsstücke an.

Paul Smith' Kreationen scheinen einer außergewöhnlichen, enzyklopädischen, intuitiven Kenntnis des äußerst stark kodifizierten Wesens des „Britischen" zu entspringen. Es ist, als verfügte er über eine innere Entsprechung der Houndsditch Clothes Exchange – kein Museum, sondern ein riesiger, alles unaufhörlich neu kombinierender Flohmarkt, in dem sich all die Artefakte seines Volkes und dessen tradierter Kultur beständig an einem wechselseitigen Austausch von Code beteiligen. Wer ein Kleidungsstück von Paul Smith sein Eigen nennt, besitzt irgendwie viel mehr als die in diesem Kleidungsstück verkörperte Gesamtsumme von Code; es ist darin eine Form der Poesie am Werk, das Gegenstück des literarischen Wissens um das Gewicht des fehlenden Wortes. Sie ist subtil und sehr stark zugleich, diese Eigenschaft, und an ihr liegt es wohl, dass sich unter meinen Lieblingskleidung der letzten zwanzig Jahre viele Kreationen von Paul Smith finden.

Ein Paar sehr dezenter mittelbrauner Brogues aus gegerbten Leder, die durch die vom Designer gewählten Sohlen – jene stark profilierten schwarzen Commandos, zu denen Skinheads greifen, wenn sie sich mit ihrer Lust auf Gewalt bei den zahmeren Doc Martens nicht gut genug aufgehoben fühlen – einen ganz neuen Dreh bekamen. Absolut perfekt. Die einzigen Schuhe, die ihnen in der Folgezeit ebenbürtig waren: Oliver Sweeneys originale Storm Derbys, die mir immer so vorkamen, als hätten sie ebenso gut von Paul Smith sein können.

Ein sehr förmliches Business-Hemd aus dem allerdunkelsten indigoblauen Denim mit Umschlagmanschetten und Haifischkragen. Wahrscheinlich das

wirkungsvollste Hemd, dass ich je besessen habe; es konnte jedem Anzug einen schrägen Touch geben und seinem Träger einem seltsam zulässigen Grad von Cowboy/Piraten-Coolness verleihen, selbst in Situationen, wo so etwas normalerweise nicht erlaubt ist.

Ein vollkommen schlichter brauner Ledergürtel, etwa Mitte der neunziger Jahre, der alles verkörpert und doch auch irgendwie übertrifft, was an der oben geschilderten amerikanischen Rekontextualisierung so toll war. Ohne Steppnähte, ein einziges Stück erstaunlich dicken und geschmeidigen Geschirrleders, an eine massive, von Hand auf alt getrimmte Rollschnalle aus Messing genietet. So einen Gürtel hinzukriegen, war das Ziel aller Hippie-Sandalenmacher in Haight-Ashbury und im East Village – ein Ziel, das sie wahrscheinlich nie erreicht haben. Das platonische Ideal eines schlichten braunen Ledergürtels, den man zu Jeans trägt.

Das „P.C.", ein Hemd aus der ersten Jahreskollektion der R. Newbold-Linie. Das typische Hemd des britischen Constables, wie man es in verfusseltem Polyester in Oxfam-Shops findet, jedoch aus dünner, grob gewebter Baumwolle, die vage an die in Indien hergestellten Uniformen der dortigen britischen Kolonialherren erinnert. Perfekt in jedem Detail bis hin zu den Doppelschlaufen zur Befestigung von Schulterklappen, aber durch den Stoff und die Wahl der Knöpfe (glatte, große, nichts sagende Plastikdinger, wie sie Schneider zur Verankerung von Hosenträgern vorsahen) auf irgendeine alternative Zeitspur verschoben. Mit seinem enorm weiten Schnitt, der bis zur Taille reichenden, verstärkten Knopfleiste und dem daran anschließenden einmal gefältelten Unterteil ist es wunderbar schlampig, wenn man es über der Hose trägt, bekommt aber etwas leicht Bedrohliches und Orwellsches, wenn man die Hemdschöße hineinsteckt.

Eine P.T.-Hose, wieder von R. Newbold. Enorm geräumig und sagenhaft bequem – normale Cargo-Hosen mit vielen Taschen wirken dagegen eng und

American teenagers wearing denim, 1950s (photo: Hulton Archive).

überladen. Baumwolldrillich, küpengefärbt in einem rauchigen, eindeutig unmilitärischen, gedeckten Burgunderrot. Eine Innenhose (ein loses Komplettfutter) aus federleichter Baumwolle sorgt bei kalter Witterung für verblüffende Wärme. Eine Krawatte aus mattem, metallisch grauem Barchent, verziert mit einem aufgebügelten Foto-Transfer-Druck von fünf Zentimeter Kantenlänge: Kühe auf einer Weide, und hinter ihnen, vor dem Horizont, dass riesige Radioteleskop von Jodrell Bank.

Ein ganz langer, ganz grüner, ganz wunderbarer Pullover, heftig betrauert, tatsächlich mein erster richtiger Kauf in der Floral Street. Ich ging am Tag nach einem Schneesturm dorthin – es war gegen Ende der achtziger Jahre – benommen vom Anblick eines London, das sich mir an diesem Tag zum ersten Mal offenbarte.

Eines London, das von seinem schmuddeligen Zaubermantel aus Schnee in eine stillere und noch geheimnisvollere Stadt als sonst verwandelt wurde.

Für mich sind England und Japan die beiden "tiefgründigsten" Nationen; eine unaufhörliche, ungeheure Faszination geht von ihnen aus. Ihre jeweiligen Kulturen sind eigentümlich kodifiziert, Bedeutungen innerhalb von Bedeutungen, bis hinunter in eine fraktale Textur, die für die meisten Einwohner beider Länder anscheinend unsichtbar ist. Inselvölker, Taschenuniversen, Psychogeographien von enormer, ununterbrochener Dauer – zwei ehemalige Empires, das britische Weltreich und das japanische Kaiserreich, zwei Zentren der Industrialisierung in ihren jeweiligen geopolitischen Arenen. (Die Japaner haben das komplette Instrumentarium der industriellen Revolution von den Briten übernommen. Haben sich absichtlich infiziert. Sind völlig außer Rand und Band geraten, zerfallen und als Asiens erste industrialisierte Nation wieder zum Vorschein gekommen.)

R. Newbold 'RC' shirt (photo: Sandro Sodano)

London und Tokio verfügen über eine gedankenlose Selbstsicherheit. Paris ist sich ständig auf narzisstische Weise seiner selbst bewusst, und New York will andauernd beglückwünscht werden. Die Einwohner von London und Tokio hegen eine ausgeprägte Wertschätzung für „geheime Marken"; sie agieren private Dramen des relativen Konsumentenstatus mit einer Ernsthaftigkeit aus, die man woanders nur selten findet. Sowohl die Engländer als auch die Japaner sind glänzende Importeure. Wenn Sie wissen wollen, welche wirklich exzellenten Produkte ihr Land hervorbringt, achten Sie darauf, was jene kleine Gruppe geradezu zwanghaft anspruchsvoller Einwohner von London und Tokio importiert. Schauen Sie sich an, worauf die Wahl des Otakus fällt, des Fanatikers der puren Information.

Zu Beginn meiner Schriftstellerlaufbahn erschienen meine Bücher im Verlag Victor Gollanz, dessen Büros in der Henrietta Street lagen. Ich lernte Covent Garden gut kennen. Eine britische „Publicity Tour" bestand in jenen Tagen größtenteils darin, in Covent Garden herumzuhängen und auf irgendwelche Journalisten und Fotografen zu warten, die sich bereit erklärt hatten zu erscheinen. Wenn ich für die nächsten ein, zwei Stunden keinen Termin hatte, konnte ich mich ein bisschen selbstständig machen. So entdeckte ich Paul Smith in seinem ordentlichen, vollen, selbst eingerichteten Ladengeschäft. Nachdem ich ungefähr in Richtung Seven Dials gewandert war, wie ich glaubte, bog ich falsch ab – da hatte ich Covent Garden noch gar nicht verlassen – und fand mich in der Floral Street wieder.

Damals gab es keinen richtigen Vertrieb für Paul-Smith-Kleidung in Kanada (und ich bin nicht einmal sicher, ob es den heute einen gibt). Die wenigen Geschäfte bei uns, die Sachen von Paul Smith führten, waren meist geradezu surrealistisch teuer, und die Händler, die seine Kreationen ins Programm nahmen, schienen eher etwas demonstrieren als sie wirklich verkaufen zu wollen. Und wie das häufig so ist, verkauften sie sich auch nicht, jedenfalls nicht zu solchen Preisen, und so konnte man sie, wenn man sehr viel Glück hatte, im Winterschlussverkauf ungefähr zum Preis normaler italienischer

Importe erstehen. Ich hatte also schon ein paar Sachen von Paul Smith (dessen Namen ich aus britischen Modezeitschriften kannte) besessen, hauptsächlich Hemden, und war von ihnen sehr angetan gewesen.

Er hatte da so eine wunderbar perverse kleine Masche mit den Manschetten. Das waren bei mir bis dahin immer Sportmanschetten gewesen, aber mit einem zusätzlichen Loch auf der Knopfseite, sodass man sie auch mit Manschettenknöpfen tragen konnte. Manschettenknöpfe waren damals in Nordamerika praktisch ausgerottet; sie galten normalerweise als ungefähr so nützlich wie Kragenknöpfe, und ich hatte durch den amerikanischen Code meiner Jugend gelernt, dass die so genannte Kombimanschette von Natur aus déclassé und höchstwahrscheinlich ein Merkmal eines minderwertigen Kleidungsstücks war. Aber Paul Smith verwendete sie. Es schien so etwas wie ein geheimes Markenzeichen zu sein, und er verwendete sie immer, außer wenn er Umschlagmanschetten benutzte. Er tat das ungeachtet des Materials, auch bei eher legeren Hemden, und gab einem damit diese skurrile verborgene Wahlmöglichkeit in Bezug auf den Stil.

Ich kann nicht mit Sicherheit sagen, dass ich den Shop in der Floral Street nach diesem Marsch durch den matschigen Londoner Schnee zum ersten Mal betrat; wahrscheinlich nicht. Aber ich begriff damals zum ersten Mal, worum es dort eigentlich ging. Vielleicht hatte ich vorher unter der Zeitverschiebung gelitten, und fast mit Sicherheit war ich von den Kennzeichen von Reichtum und modischer Eleganz – oder was ich dafür hielt – eingeschüchtert gewesen, weil ich beides nicht besaß.

Doch als ich an diesem Tag durch Zufall auf den Laden stieß, schien er mir ein Wunder im besten Sinne zu sein (und das ist er tatsächlich auch).

Ich fühlte mich an gewisse äußerst gediegene, ungeheuer altmodische Geschäfte in Barcelona und Rom Ende der sechziger Jahre erinnert - derart viktorianische Geschäfte, dass sie noch nicht einmal dazu übergegangen waren, ihr Angebot öffentlich zur Schau zu stellen. Wenn man dort nach Strümpfen fragte, holte jemand welche aus nummerierten Eichenkästen, die eine ganze Wand einnahmen. Weil der Shop in der Floral Street eine Collage viktorianischer Ladeneinrichtungen ist, und obwohl natürlich einige Sachen ausgestellt werden, gehört er für mich irgendwie in diesen Kontext nummerierter Kisten. Er war einer der schönsten Läden, die ich je gesehen hatte, und das ist er auch heute noch.

Und wie um mir jedes etwa noch vorhandene Zögern auszutreiben, lief gerade der Winterschlussverkauf. Massen von Menschen brachten die zusammengelegten Hemden durcheinander und wühlten in den Krawatten auf den Tischen, und ich hatte das Gefühl, dass ich es ebenfalls gefahrlos tun konnte. Also tat ich es.

Schließlich kam ich, nachdem ich mich von oben bis unten durch den ganzen Laden gearbeitet hatte, mit diesem wundervollen Zopfmuster-Pullover aus sehr schwerer Baumwolle im schönsten, leuchtendsten Dunkelgrün wieder heraus. Anschließend zog ich ihn eine ganze Weile praktisch gar nicht mehr aus. Und dann übernahm ihn meine Frau und erkor ihn zu einem ihrer bequemen Lieblingsstücke, und sie trug ihn noch einige Jahre bei der Gartenarbeit, bis er, glaube ich, buchstäblich auseinanderfiel.

Ich mag Stil, aber nicht immer die Mode, und ein großer Designer – insbesondere auf dem Gebiet der Herrenmode – ist für mich in erster Linie jemand, der ganz spezielle, unvergessliche Kleidungsstücke zustande bringt, die auf genau diese Weise zu Favoriten werden. Dinge, die man nach dem Kauf nicht irgendwo ablegt, sondern immer um sich hat, bis sie auseinander fallen. Wie selten so etwas ist.

Paul Smith hat das, glaube ich, schon immer getan. Seine Kreationen sind auf eine Art persönlich, die wir im Allgemeinen nicht mit Designern englischer Muttersprache verbinden (und wenn doch, sind sie fast unweigerlich britisch).

Was Paul Smith in meinen Augen jedoch immer von anderen Modeschöpfern – auch anderen britischen Modeschöpfern – unterschieden hat, ist diese Aura der inneren Houndsditch Clothes Exchange. Dieser rekombinanten Modebibliothek von Babel, in der alle Texte mit allen anderen zusammenströmen und das „Neue" unmittelbar und genau nach Plan aus den komplizierten und miteinander verknüpften Code-Mengen entsteht, die einer ja schließlich sehr alten und komplizierten Kultur zugrunde liegen und sie erschaffen. In der das „Neue" im Kontext entsteht.

Womit übrigens nicht gesagt sein soll, dass Paul Smith nur der Schöpfer von Markenklassikern mit einem kleinen Kniff ist – von solide gefertigten, ziemlich teuren Dingen, die man jahrelang ganz besonders schätzt. Das ist er natürlich auch, aber es sind immer noch ein paar andere kleine Provokationen im Spiel, und in der Tat entwirft er häufig Sachen, die mir abstrakt gefallen, die ich jedoch nicht sonderlich gern tragen würde. Ich fühle mich nicht sehr wohl in übermäßig provokanter Kleidung, und Paul Smith zeigt bei manchen seiner Kreationen immer wieder eine Art genialer Duchampscher Wildheit. (Die Surrealisten waren zu ihrer Zeit fast ausnahmslos als große Dandys bekannt.)

Diese Seite von Paul Smith ist in meinen Augen das Resultat einer bewussten Vergrößerung der Bandbreite, der Einbeziehung „fremder" Codes. Und damit meine ich nicht nur Kleidungscodes, sondern Codes des gesamten menschlichen Universums künstlich hergestellter Dinge. Sie oder ich könnten in Indien einen Tresen aus abgenutztem blauem Laminat sehen. Ich glaube, Paul Smith sieht bei einem Blick auf denselben Tresen manchmal ein Hemd oder einen Stoff, aus dem man ein Hemd machen sollte.

Sichtbare Schlüssel dafür, was in dieser Hinsicht in ihm abläuft, könnten jene einzigartigen Produkte und Artefakte sein, die er auf seinen Einkaufsreisen entdeckt und die man manchmal faszinierender- und verblüffenderweise in seinen Läden findet. Sehr seltsame und (in einem imaginierten ursprünglichen Kontext) ganz normale und wunderbare Dinge, die uns das Auge des Designers offenbart – und die uns offenbaren, was für ein Auge dieser Designer hat.

Ich vermute auf der Grundlage der käuflichen Objekte aus Japan, auf die man in Paul Smiths Läden stößt, dass ein Paul-Smith-Fotoalbum von Tokio genau das Bild von Tokio zeigen würde, das ich flüchtig gesehen habe, aber nie auf Fotos bannen konnte. Tatsächlich hat mir Paul Smiths Eindruck von Tokio ein solches Bild vermittelt, bevor ich selbst dorthin gereist bin, und als ich es schließlich tat, sah ich sofort, dass Paul Smith es hundertprozentig getroffen hatte.

Und irgendwo in Tokio, erklärte mir mein Reiseführer bei jenem ersten Besuch, habe es zu Ehren des großen Paul Smith eine Ausstellung seiner Kreationen sowie seltener und in den Augen der Japaner durch und durch britischer Objekte gegeben. Das beliebteste davon, so teilte mir mein Übersetzer mit, sei einer jener außergewöhnlichen Mini-Sportwagen. Ich hatte einmal einen auf der Autobahn gesehen, einen seltsamen Traum mit ledernen Kühlerhaubengurten wie aus einem Fantasy-Roman von Michael Moorcock; sein einsames Hinterrad hatte einen prächtigen Pfauenschwanz aus Regen aufgeworfen. Damals lernte ich auch (obwohl ich es inzwischen wieder vergessen habe) das japanische Wort für „sich danach sehnen, etwas zu sein, was man von Natur aus nicht sein kann". Ich glaube, man erläuterte es mir im Kontext einer Erklärung, welche Anziehungskraft Paul Smith und der verrückte, wunderschöne Mini auf die Japaner ausüben.

Aber ich wollte nie Brite sein, und ich glaube auch nicht, dass Paul Smiths japanische Fans Briten sein wollen. Für mich, und ich glaube auch für sie, geht es um die Codes. Um seine Houndsditch Exchange. Seine Beherrschung der Tiefencodes, in der ihm aller Wahrscheinlichkeit nach niemand gleichkommt.

Jahre sind vergangen, seit ich diese Hemden mit dem verborgenen zusätzlichen Knopfloch entdeckt habe, und Paul Smith ist für mich der interessanteste Modeschöpfer geblieben. Weil er in dem erstaunlich restringierten, aber endlos

rekombinanten Code von Stoff, Textur, Farbe und Schnitt weiterhin etwas artikuliert, etwas so Komplexes wie eine ganze Kultur.

Als ich letztes Jahr, vom Jetlag gepeinigt, in der sommerlichen Dunkelheit vor der Morgendämmerung von meinem Hotel in Notting Hill Richtung Portobello wanderte, stieß ich zum ersten Mal auf Paul Smiths Laden in Westbourne Grove. Er schwebte dort an seiner Ecke, die wunderschön illuminierten Fenster eingepasst ins Gefüge des in sich selbst versunkenen, unauflöslichen Rätsels, das London ist. Wieder einmal perfekt, und perfekt gelegen im Netz dieses Rätsels, ganz in der Nähe von Portobello Market, wo die Codes zahlloser künstlicher Dinge zu dieser Stunde, in der Dunkelheit verschlossener Glaskästen in hundert provisorischen Einkaufspassagen, in prachtvoller Komplexität kommunizieren.

Sumo wrestler pencil, on Paul Smith's desk, Floral Street, London (photo: Robert Violette).
Mini Cooper car customised by Paul Smith (photo: Sandro Sodano).
Paul Smith shop, Westbourne House, Notting Hill Gate, London (photo: Sonia Peric).

A hundred and fifty years ago, there lay, adjacent to the southern boundary of the City of London, near the south end of Petticoat Lane, a rectangular plank enclosure of roughly an acre of dank and barren ground. This was the Houndsditch Clothes Exchange, where dealers sat on benches before soiled heaps of boots, clothing, umbrellas, whips, and every other sort of worn and discarded article. Here stolen garments were 'translated' (their labels and any markings removed), and worn but better-quality clothing was sold on to backstreet tradesmen, who might assemble one waistcoat from the remains of two, or work temporary miracles on ruined boots. This unsavoury and Dickensian establishment had, in retrospect, more to do with the future of British men's clothing than any activity of the smart tailors of the day.

The translators who bought from Houndsditch were unknowingly engaged in a peculiarly modern activity, recombining codes of cut and fabric to produce garments that had not previously existed. If the new factories of the Victorian Age introduced the modern means of production, the ragmen of Houndsditch and their professional clientèle, the translators, prefigure the recombinant impulse that has been one of the two key factors in the history of twentieth-century clothing design.

The other factor, of course, has been military clothing and workwear, the two World Wars having introduced the means of accurate proportional sizing, ergonomic design, and a rational, apparently design-free non-aesthetic. And really, between these two, there's been little else genuinely new; little else that a Victorian tailor might find utterly incomprehensible. Subtract recombinant design, our endless postmodern mining of the substrate codes, subtract the influence of workwear and military surplus, and one's left with a tired simulacrum of traditional British men's tailoring.

Think of the state of British men's fashion at the end of the last war, just prior to the emergence of new paradigms. There was really only the demob suit, and a few fringe bohemians of New Edwardian cut, whose codes were already in process of being inherited by the Teds. In America, at the same time, men were being sold an irony-free fantasy of quasi-Englishness, courtesy of Brooks Bros and their countless imitators.

Moss Bros and Brooks Bros and in between the grey Atlantic.

My American boyhood abounded in button-downs (originally a raffish collar-modification appropriated from British polo-players) and accessories in 'regimental' stripes. A sort of humourless hash of borrowed code, bodged together in the service of a weird and spurious nostalgia for New England (where it was enormously powerful and popular, as it was in the South where I grew up, and remains so to this day). Ivy League was all there was, at least on the 'better' side of the tracks, and it was back to this prelapsarian American Eden that Ralph Lauren, a very long decade or so later, would eventually lead the Sixties-frazzled remnants of my generation of Americans, doing hugely well for himself in the process.

Then, in the mid-1960s, something began to happen in England, amid a tiny, infinitely élitist circle of Soho style-otakus, something that brought the Ivy League code looping back into the nation that had produced its parent memes. In a series of inspired reappropriations by these modernist fanatics, these ur-Mods, the American button-down was imported to England, almost covertly, along with khaki trousers, Gold Cup socks and Bass Weejuns, and was utterly recontextualised. In the hands of these gimlet-eyed, detail-crazed obsessives, elements of a self-consciously Anglo-inflected Americana were sent out on a cultural mission that my

Tulane students, Louisiana, c. 1956 (photo: Hulton Archive).
'The Houndsditch Macaroni', 1772, J. Bretherton (photo: Guildhall Library, Corporation of London).
British soldiers, 1915 (photo: Mary Evans Picture Library).
Teddy boys, 1950s (photo: Hulton Archive).

schoolmates and I could never have comprehended. In the context of mid-1960s London, these clothes meant something else, something entirely and brilliantly new. They became the crucial gesture of a very genuine sort of independence, the roots of an impulse my American friends and I were unlikely to encounter until we saw Michael Caine in 'The Ipcress File', exhibiting a pared-down Cockney cool we could only marvel at.

In America, meanwhile, we were finding our way out of those very styles, so different in meaning in their original context. We were discovering the beauties of the Army-Navy store, where perfect, perfectly inexpensive chambray workshirts were to be found, and Levi's in the classic sense, and square-buckled leather garrison-belts, and much else as well. The dawn of this American recontextualisation was very much about newness and discovery. I've never accepted Tom Wolfe's view that what we were about was a pathetic borrowing of the balls of the labouring classes.

I doubt Tom Wolfe ever owned a pair of Levi's, even when Levi's were Levi's. And today the Japanese own the original looms that produced the denim of the Levi's I remember, and if I want to reexperience those, I must buy either French or Dutch jeans, assembled in Tunisia, from fabric that is woven exclusively in Japan.

In any case, it didn't last very long, that first flash of recontextualisation, in America. It was soon drowned in a loopy sea of fringe and crystals, and, to some extent, in the product of London's Carnaby Street, a short-lived impulse that had some several of its roots in that original British recontextualisation.

But both of these brief stylistic periods, on both sides of the Atlantic, have continued to deeply influence global style. That is why you see young men in Tokyo who still go to great pains to wear exactly what Steve McQueen

Steve McQueen, 'The Great Escape', 1963
(photo: Mirisch/United Artists, courtesy The Kobal Collection).

wore in 'The Great Escape', and that is why the Polo website offers used vintage 'classics' at several times the cost of Mr Lauren's often quite meticulous reproductions of those same garments.

Then Paul Smith came along. Paul Smith's designs seem to emanate from some extraordinary and encyclopaedic awareness of the intensely codified nature of 'Britishness'. It is as though he possesses some inner equivalent of the Houndsditch Clothes Exchange – not a museum but a vast, endlessly recombinant jumble sale, in which all of the artefacts of his nation and culture constantly engage in a mutual exchange of code. To possess a Paul Smith garment is to possess far more, somehow, than the sum total of code embodied in that garment. There is a species of poetry at work here, the equivalent of the literary awareness of the weight of the absent word. It is at once subtle and very strong, this quality, and to it I attribute the fact that many of my favourite garments, bought over the past twenty years, were designed by Paul Smith.

A pair of intensely reserved mid-brown pebble-grain brogues, torqued into something else entirely by the designer's choice of soles: the same lug-toothed black Commando's chosen by skinheads unwilling to trust the intensity of their bother to the more tender mercies of Dr Marten's. Absolutely perfect. The only shoe to match them, subsequently: Oliver Sweeney's original 'Storm Derby', a shoe which always seemed to me as though it might have been designed by Paul Smith.

A very formal business shirt, French cuffs, spread collar, executed in the darkest of indigo denims. This was possibly the single most effective shirt I've ever owned, able to detourne any suit and lend to the wearer a strangely admissible degree of cowboy/pirate cool, even in situations where same is not ordinarily permitted.

A perfectly plain brown leather belt, mid-1990s, that embodies and yet somehow surpasses everything that was great about the American re-contextualisation described above. Unstitched, a single length of astonishingly thick and supple harness-leather, riveted to a hand-distressed heavy-duty brass roller-buckle. This is the belt that hippie sandal-makers in places like Haight-Ashbury and the East Village were striving to make but probably never did. It is the Platonic ideal of a plain brown leather belt to wear with jeans.

The 'P. C.', a shirt from the first year's range of the R. Newbold line. The British police constable's shirt, exactly as encountered in pilled polyester in Oxfam shops, but rendered in a thin, coarsely-woven cotton faintly suggestive of the Indian-made uniforms of the Raj. Complete in every detail, down to the double loops for anchoring shoulderboards, but skewed into some alternate time-track by fabric and choice of buttons (smooth large featureless plastic of the sort tailors provided to comfortably anchor trouser-braces). Hugely cut, with a placket front opening to a one-pleat shirtwaist, it's brilliantly sloppy if worn with the tails out, yet faintly menacing and Orwellian when worn with them tucked.

'P. T.' trousers, again from R. Newbold. Vastly capacious, absurdly comfortable, these make ordinary multi-pocket cargo pants look tense and overwrought. Cotton drill, vat-dyed a smoky, decidedly unmilitary shade of muted burgundy. A secondary, inner pair of pants (a loose integral liner) made of handkerchief-weight cotton, provides startling warmth in cold weather.

A tie, in dull, gunmetal fustian, emblazoned with a two-inch-square iron-on photographic transfer of cows, in a meadow, and behind them, against the horizon, the great radio telescope at Jodrell Bank.

R. Newbold, 'P.C.' shirt (photo: Sandro Sodano).

A very long, very green, very wonderful pullover, much lamented, that was actually my first real purchase in Paul Smith's Floral Street shop. I went there the day after a snowstorm, in the later 1980s, stunned at the revelation of a London I'd never seen before. A quiet and more than usually mysterious London, under its tatty but powerfully transformative fabric of snow.

England and Japan are to my mind the two 'deepest' nations, the most endlessly and perfectly fascinating. Their respective cultures are peculiarly codified, meaning within meaning, down into a fractal texture apparently invisible to most natives of either country. Island nations, pocket universes, psychogeographies of tremendous and unbroken duration, they are seats of former empire and points for the emergence of industrialisation in their respective geopolitical arenas. (The Japanese bought the complete Industrial Revolution kit from the British. Infected themselves deliberately. Went mad. Fell apart. Emerged as Asia's first industrialised nation.)

London and Tokyo possess an unthinking self-assurance. Paris is perpetually and narcissistically conscious of itself, and New York needs forever to be congratulated. The inhabitants of London and Tokyo, however, are consummate appreciators of 'secret brands'; they act out private dramas of relative consumer-status with a gravitas seldom seen elsewhere. Both the English and the Japanese are brilliant importers. If you want to know what it is that your own country produces that is genuinely excellent, look for what the most obsessively discerning residents of London and Tokyo choose to import. Look for the choices of the otaku, the fanatic of pure information.

My publishers, at the start of my career as a novelist, were Victor Gollancz, whose offices were in Henrietta Street. I came to know Covent Garden well. A British 'publicity tour', in those days, consisted largely of hanging about Covent Garden, waiting for whichever journalists and photographers agreed to show up. If I had no appointments for the next hour or so, I could branch out a bit, and that was how I first discovered Paul Smith in his proper, full, self-generated retail setting. Having wandered, one snowy day, in the approximate direction of Seven Dials, I took a wrong turn, and found myself in Floral Street.

At that time there was no proper distributor of Paul Smith clothing in Canada, where I have lived most of my life (and I'm not certain there is even now). What little Paul Smith reached retail outlets here tended to be quite surrealistically expensive, and any retailer who stocked it seemed more determined to make a point than actually to sell it. And often, in the way of things, it didn't sell, not at those prices, and could be had in January if one was very lucky, at something like the price of ordinary Italian imports. So I had had a few things by Paul Smith, whose name I knew from British style magazines; mostly shirts, and I had liked them very much.

Paul Smith did this tiny, wonderfully perverse thing with his shirt cuffs. All of which for me, so far, had been barrel cuffs, but with an extra hole on the button side, allowing them to be worn with cufflinks. Cufflinks at that point in North America were virtually extinct, about as useful ordinarily as collar-studs, and I had been taught via the American code of my youth that the so-called 'convertible' cuff was inherently déclassé, and very probably the mark of an inferior garment. But Paul Smith put them on. It seemed to be a sort of secret trademark, and he always did it, unless the cuffs were French. He did it regardless of the fabric or relative informality of a particular shirt, and thereby gave you this quirky hidden style-option.

I can't say for certain that this visit through the slushy London snow was my first experience of the Floral Street shop, and in fact I suspect it wasn't. But it was the first time I 'got' it, really. Perhaps, before, I'd been jetlagged, and almost certainly intimidated by what I took to be the markers of wealth and fashionability, neither of which I possessed.

On that day, however, encountering it by accident, it seemed (as actually it is) a most benevolent marvel.

I was reminded of certain very sedate, hugely old-fashioned shops in Barcelona and Rome, in the late 1960s. Places so Victorian that they had not yet come around to the overt display of goods. Where, if you inquired about socks, someone fetched them out for you from a wall of numbered oaken hutches. Because the Floral Street store is a collage of Victorian shopfittings, and though things are certainly displayed, it is somehow within that same context of numbered hutches. It seemed one of the best-looking shops I had ever seen, and indeed it still does.

And, as if to put paid to any lingering hesitation I might have felt, the January sales were on. Crowds were mussing the folded shirts and pawing through tables of ties, and I felt that I might safely do so too. And I did.

Emerging, eventually, having rooted my way top to bottom through the whole shop, with this wonderful green pullover, very heavy cable-knit cotton, in the most beautiful and vibrant shade of dark green. I seldom took it off, for quite a while after. And then my wife took it over, and it became a favourite comfortable thing of hers, and she wore it for years more, gardening, until it literally, I imagine, fell apart. I love style and don't always like fashion, and my idea of a great designer, and particularly a designer of men's clothing, is in large part of someone capable of producing very special, very memorable garments that become favourites in exactly that way. Items that are never abandoned, once purchased, but which stick around to fall apart. How rare that is.

Paul Smith, I think, has been doing it all along. His designs are personal in a way that we generally don't associate with designers for whom English is a

Paul Smith shop, Floral Street, Covent Garden, London (photos: Mat Buck).

first language (and if we do, they tend almost invariably to be British). What has always set Paul Smith apart, for me, from other designers, even other British designers, is that sense of the inner Houndsditch Clothes Exchange. That recombinant sartorial Library of Babel, in which all texts flow into all other texts, and the 'new' arrives directly and very much on schedule from the intricate and interlocking shoals of code that underlie what is, after all, a most ancient and intricate culture. In which the 'new' arrives 'in context'.

Which is not to suggest, by the way, that Paul Smith is the creator merely of trademark classics-plus-quirk – of solidly-made, rather expensive things that one treasures for years. He is that, of course, but there is always another edge or three in play, and indeed he frequently designs things that I enjoy in the abstract but wouldn't particularly care to wear. I am not at ease wearing excessively edgy clothing, and Paul Smith, in some of his designs, continues to manifest a species of genial Duchampian ferocity. (The Surrealists were known in their day, almost to a man, for being great dandies.)

This side of Paul Smith I take to be the result of a deliberate widening of bandwidth, embracing 'alien' codes. Not just codes of dress, but codes of the whole human universe of manufactured objects. You or I, in India, might see a countertop of worn blue laminate. I think Paul Smith looks at that same counter and sometimes sees a shirt, or a fabric from which a shirt should be made.

Visible keys to this part of his process, perhaps, are those singular products and artefacts, discovered by Paul Smith on his own retail journey, which one is sometimes intrigued and baffled to find in his shops. Very strange and ordinary (in some imagined original context) and wonderful things, both revealed by, and revealing of, the designer's eye.

I suspect, on the basis of the Japanese retail objects encountered in his shops, that a Paul Smith snapshot-album of Tokyo would reveal the very Tokyo that I have glimpsed but never managed to take snapshots of. Indeed, Paul Smith's sense of Tokyo gave me some sense of it before I had actually gone there, and when I did go there, I saw immediately that he had been spot on.

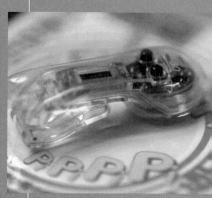

And somewhere in Tokyo, my guide informed me on that first visit, there had been mounted, in honour of the great Paul Smith, a display of his designs, and also of what were deemed to be rare and quintessentially British objects. The most popular of these, my translator informed me, had been one of those extraordinary Mini Cooper sports cars, emblazened with the Paul Smith multi-stripe. I had glimpsed a Mini once on a motorway, a strange dream with leather bonnet-straps, like a car out of a Michael Moorcock fantasy, its rear wheels throwing up a gorgeous roostertail of rain. I was also told, then, though I have since forgotten it, the Japanese word that means 'longing to be that which one by nature cannot be'. This was explained to me, I believe, in the context of an explanation of Paul Smith's appeal to the Japanese, and that mad beautiful Mini's appeal.

But I have never wanted to be British, and I do not think that Paul Smith's Japanese fans want to be British either. For me, as I believe for them, it is the codes that fascinate. His Houndsditch Exchange. His mastery of the deep codes, in which he very probably has no equal.

Japanese ear alarm and Sumo wrestler pencil, on Paul Smith's desk, Floral Street, London (photos: Robert Violette).

Years have passed since I first discovered those shirts with the covert extra button-hole, and Paul Smith has remained for me the most interesting of designers. Because he continues to articulate something as complex as an entire culture in the remarkably restricted, yet endlessly recombinant, code of fabric and texture and colour and cut.

Last year, wandering jetlagged in predawn summer darkness towards the Portobello Road from my Notting Hill hotel, I came upon Paul Smith's Westbourne Grove shop for the first time. I saw it floating there on its corner, beautifully illuminated windows set into the texture of the self-involved and inexplicable mystery that is London. Perfect, once again, and perfectly situated in the grid of that mystery, just off Portobello Market, where the codes of countless man-made things communicate in glorious complexity, at that hour, in the darkness of locked glass cases in a hundred makeshift arcades.

Mini Cooper car customised by Paul Smith (photo: Sandro Sodano).
Paul Smith shop, Westbourne House, Notting Hill Gate, London (photo: Sonia Peric).

122

Paul Smith

nottingham

My dad's father, Benjamin Smith, and my parents, Harold and Marjorie
Irene Smith, on their wedding day in Nottingham, April 1932.

Home in Nottingham was always very comfortable. I had my own bedroom in my parents' house and went through the usual decorating bit – thought I was an artist for about a year and so had a lot of dreadful things on the wall called 'art'. Excellent mum, quirky dad – an always stable, good relationship. Lots of energy from my dad, lots of tranquillity from my mum. My dad, Harold, who was a draper and an amateur photographer, had an easy-going personality and I hope that I have inherited that from him. He could walk into a room and within a few minutes make everyone there feel completely at ease. So I believe in sincerity. It is very rare. We can all be programmed into saying what people want to hear. I believe in effort, in always trying at the things you do and I believe in the power of personality.

When I look back, I realise how influenced I was by Nottingham. I'd cycle around – there'd be the coal miners, Derby tweeds and the elegance of country squires. My brother worked for the Post Office and wore that blue cotton drill GPO shirt.

There was also an amazing mix of the classes in Nottingham. I still go back there nearly every week, because the head office of the business is up there, as well as my shop.

I grew up about four miles outside Nottingham, went to a secondary modern school and left at 15. I loathed school, I couldn't concentrate. When I left school my father asked me what I wanted to do and I said, 'I want to be a racing cyclist'. He said 'There's no money in that, what do you really want to do?' He happened to know a man who ran a clothing warehouse, and they employed me to run errands. The only thing that appealed to me was that it was about four miles from home and I could cycle there and back every day. I had no interest whatsoever in their clothes, which were fairly good quality, but it was like a production line. Then when I was 17 I had a bad crash on my bike, which left me in hospital for three months. During that time I realised that there might be something else in the world apart from cycling.

When I got out of hospital I discovered the English – before then I'd never really had a social life outside of cycling. Just by chance I met a lot of people from the art college and became interested in things like art and fashion, and back at the warehouse I started to make displays in its showroom. Even though they were basic clothes, I'd get a shirt and a jacket together and make a display, and it would suddenly sell better. The boss was really impressed, and he gave me all the buying to do for the menswear when I was still only 17. I left the warehouse when a girl I knew from the art college wanted to open her own shop. She asked me if I'd like to help her. I found the premises, decorated them, organised the lease – I'd never done any of that before but I was so enthusiastic. I still am. I ran the whole shop for six years and that's how I started. The shop was successful for a long time afterwards, too.

From the age of 18 to 20 I went the opposite way to my previous pure child self. Basically, I got drunk and discovered 'sex, drugs and rock and roll'.

This was the late Sixties, remember. You wore hair that's too long, 19 scarves, flowery shirts, velvet trousers, or whatever was shocking at the time. I was once stopped in the street by an elderly gentleman who was outraged by what I was wearing. He said: 'I fought in the war for you and you dress like a bloody girl!' I think he was probably quite right. But then, after the hippie phase, I went more bespoke – suits in mint green or blue, made-to-measure boots with Cuban heels and a simple black cashmere sweater. Or I'd wear Levi's 501s, which you couldn't buy in Britain at the time. They were expensive, but somehow I'd find the money.

I lived with my parents until I was 21, until 1967, when I moved in with Pauline Denyer. She was a designer, teaching fashion two days a week. She is now a painter. I was still working as the manager of that clothes shop. I fell in love with Pauline immediately – it was wonderful then, and it has been wonderful ever since. We had a beautiful flat, a huge thing in Nottingham, and we were there for a fair amount of time. Then we actually bought our first house. The current house we own, in London, we've had for more than ten years, and it's great. Pauline has her own studio and can paint there.

Having a long relationship with Pauline has not only been lovely, but it has stabilised my life. It means I'm not looking, not searching, for anything. I'm not always changing my character in order to attract other people. We'd rather talk about the garden than whether or not we're on the cover of a magazine (that's just part of the job). Pauline's not only very clear about who I am and what I am, but, in a design and business sense, she's been more helpful than anyone I've ever worked with. I couldn't have done any of this without her. She opened up the London fashion world for me at a different level. That was key. She's been key in everything I've ever done. She gave me the confidence to go for it, to branch out on my own. She realised that I had all this energy and enthusiasm. She fostered that, channelled it. And

With my grandfather at the seaside, 1949.

Some portraits of me as a schoolboy in the 1950s, taken by my father, including one outside the gates of Nottingham University; sunbathing with friends in Nottinghamshire; at home with a toy petrol station; Dad being his usual self at the seaside, in Dorset; and me at the Bristol docks in 1953. Later he wrote on the back of that photograph: 'Paul – You said to me "I wish I could go on the sea in that boat – all over the world" – you've done it by air! – Dad'.

without discussion, it was menswear, simple as that. I'd been responsible for buying it, so now I suppose I thought I should design it. In those days I obviously had no idea about design, as I'd had no formal training, I just picked things up as I went along. Pauline actually designed all of the early collections.

I opened my first shop in 1970, but only for two days a week. The other days I did anything to make a buck to run the shop on my terms. I earned money any way I could. At that time, the key word was 'individualism', and that was what we were all trying to be, individualist. In those days the key to being a successful designer was creating clothes which had character, which made you look different from everyone else. This is what I was trying to do when I first opened, and I guess it worked. People would come from all over, from Newcastle, Glasgow, Sheffield, Leeds, to buy clothes from the shop because they couldn't get anything like them anywhere else. We were a little oasis outside London.

With my father on the Clifton Suspension Bridge, Bristol.

This was the set up for a photograph my dad staged so that it would appear as though I was flying a carpet over the Brighton Pavilion. Later on, my father wrote on the back of this photo (right): '"Flying Carpet" set-up in the garden. All the background, woodwork and boxes, etc, were painted out on negative, just leaving Paul and carpet. Picture was on 2 1/4" negative on my Rolleiflex camera (also the second negative, taken at Brighton). Brighton enlarged first (shading a spot in the sky ready for carpet). Change negative + lens, shade rest of picture, + expose 2nd neg."

My dad inscribed the picture on the left, 'Smart from the Start', Skegness, around 1963. Above: with school friends; me at the wheel of my dad's car; at a family gathering photographed by Mr. Albert Moore. I'm standing on the right – inscribed on the back by my father: 'That was a Happy Christmas at Skegness'.

I don't normally prefer old things to new things, but cars are different: modern cars tend to have rather square designs, whereas vintage Fifties cars have a beautifully rounded shape. And I like their character. Here I am with a Hillman in the mid 1960s. Now I own a beautiful 1955 Bristol 405, which has a delicious steering-wheel, with little notches for all your fingers. There's only one dial on the dashboard, rather than all those discotheque light shows you get on modern cars. People expect me to know all about how my car works, but, in fact, I barely know where to put the keys. I don't even know how fast my Bristol goes: I've only ever driven it in London.

Me on the telephone in my first shop; and, on the left, Barry Brooke, a founding director of Paul Smith Limited, with Stuart and Ron at the Pushpin Gallery in the basement of my shop at 6 Byard Lane in Nottingham, some time in the early 1970s.

I love life. I feel very privileged. I sometimes think I'm going to step into the street and get hit by a bus because I've had so many brilliant days for so long. I think: 'Why have I been so lucky?' I never assume anything. I never assume that I'm always going to be healthy, or happy, or that business is always going to be successful. Those things, and Pauline, keep me grounded.

With Pauline in Italy, in the early 1970s.

Harold Smith

fig.01

My late father, Harold Smith (1903-1998), by profession a credit draper in
Nottingham, was a passionate amateur photographer and a co-founder of the
Beeston Camera Club. When he wasn't supplying clothes and household goods direct
to people's homes, he thought about composition, light, witty juxtapositions,
experiment -- not only taking photographs but also developing and printing all
his own work in his home-made attic darkroom. In contrast, my photographs with
an instant camera are about observation, humour and the 'caught moment'. Very
different in some ways from my father's photographs, but oddly, strongly similar.

fig.01 PAUL SMITH AND HAROLD SMITH, 1997 (photo: Doug Marke)

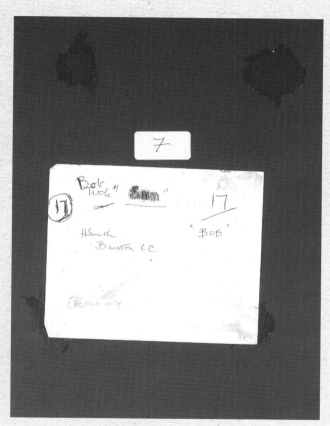

fig.02

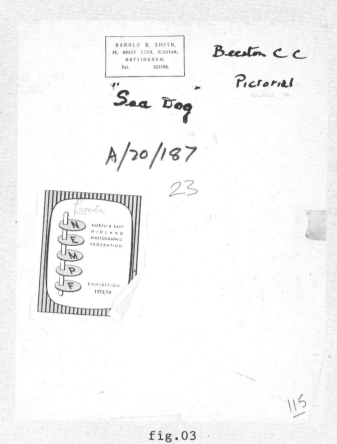

fig.03

fig.02 BOB LITTLE (verso) fig.03 SEA DOG (verso)

fig.04   fig.05

fig.04 SEA DOG fig.05 BOB LITTLE

fig.06

fig.07

fig.06 BROWNIE   fig.07 EASTERN OUTLOOK

fig.08   fig.09

fig.08 EASTERN OUTLOOK (verso)   fig.09 BROWNIE (verso)

fig.10 UNTITLED (verso)

fig.11 UNTITLED

SEA MIST CORNWALL

fig.12

fig.13

fig.12 SEA-MIST fig.13 MOONWOOD

$^{19}\!/_{20}$ 42

fig.14

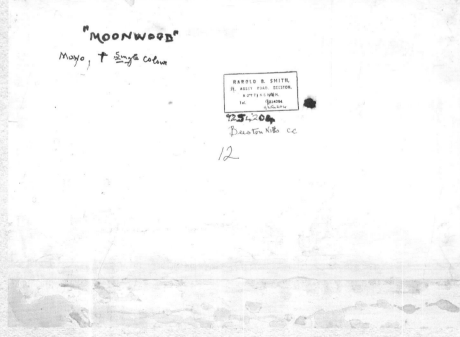

"MOONWOOD"

Mono, + Single colour

9234204

Beeston Notts CC

12

fig.15

fig.14 SEA-MIST (verso)   fig.15 MOONWOOD (verso)

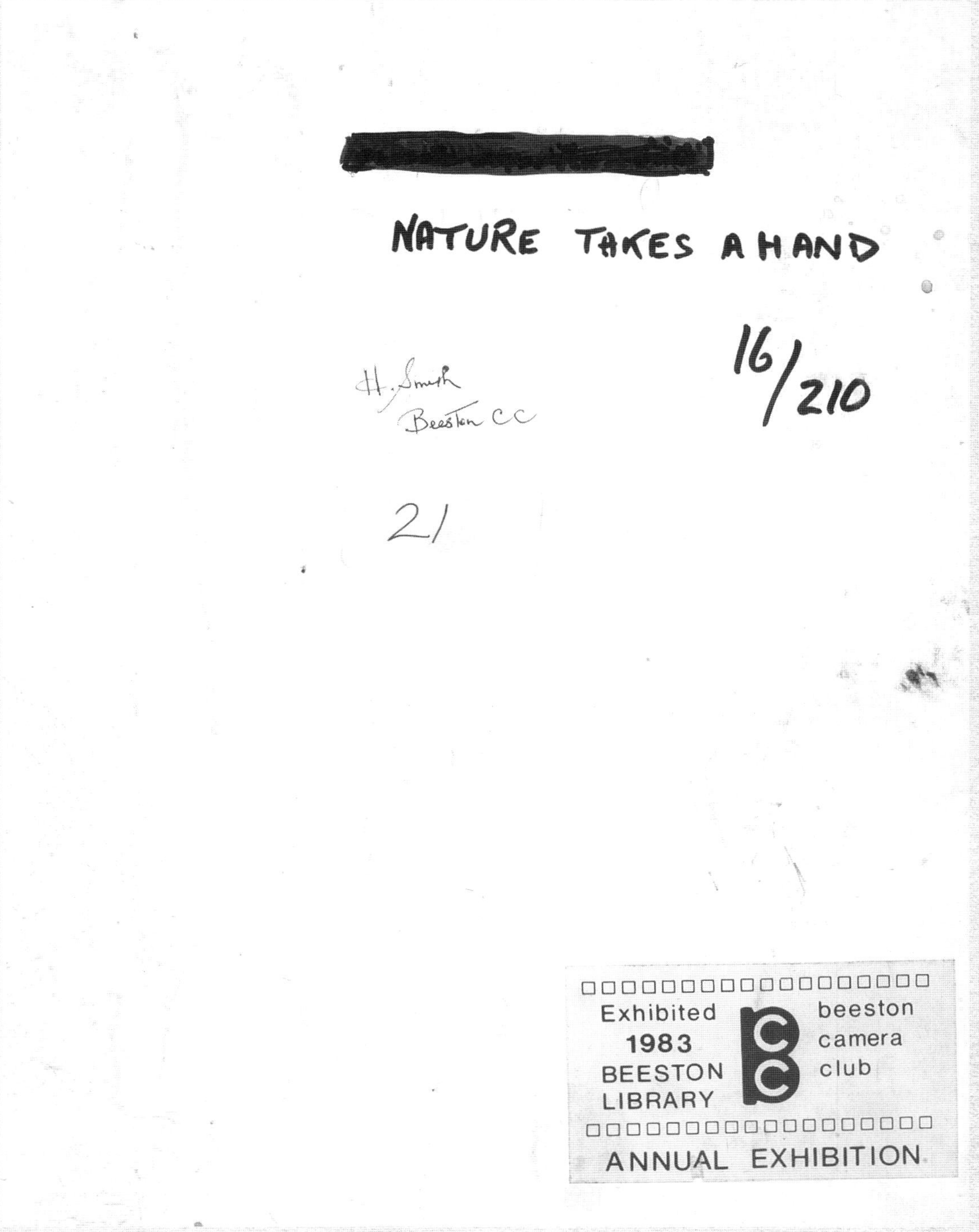

NATURE TAKES A HAND

16/210

H. Smith
Beeston CC

21

fig.16 NATURE TAKES A HAND (verso)

fig.17 NATURE TAKES A HAND

fig.18 SAFE DRIVER

fig.19 SAFE DRIVER (verso)

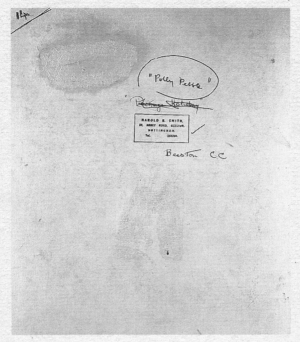

fig.20

fig.21

fig.20 POLLY PEBBLE (verso) fig.21 HOLD MY HAND LOVE (verso)

fig.22

fig.23

fig.22 POLLY PEBBLE   fig.23 HOLD MY HAND LOVE

In November 2000 there was a small exhibition in Tokyo, called 'Father + Son', of my photographs and my father's. At the opening, the Japanese guests kept coming up to me and saying 'Same DNA! Same DNA!'

round the bend
richard williams

He remembers nothing before his eleventh birthday…

…just the quiet blur of a contented suburban childhood. Then his father gave him the racing bike.

It was a pale blue machine called a Paramount, made by a small company a few miles from his home, on the other side of the city. It had belonged to a racing cyclist who had sold it to his father. The frame of the bike was too big but he rode it anyway, feeling the unfamiliar sensitivity of the pull brakes, and learning how to use the lever to change the derailleur gears without graunching the chain as it slipped across the silver cogs. There is a picture of him astride it, in the garden of the house, wearing his school uniform.

On Wednesday evenings after school he used to go with his father to the British Legion, where members of the camera club met. There he learnt about the masters of photography, about the 'ad lib' style of Henri Cartier-Bresson and about how Edward Weston used slow shutter speeds to photograph water. A little way along the corridor, in the British Legion building, the meetings of the cycling club were also held. Through them he started spending his Thursday nights listening to the older members of the club as they told stories of other masters, men with

sun-blackened faces and haunted eyes and lean bodies and names that an English schoolboy found hard to pronounce – Jacques Anquetil, Louison Bobet, Raymond Poulidor, Fausto Coppi. He heard about their battles in the Alps and the Pyrenees, how they flew up mountains called the Galibier and the Tourmalet, and how they hurtled down again in terrifying descents that sometimes ended in tangled metal and bloody wounds.

He liked hearing about these races through the villages and small towns of France and Italy. Geography was something he enjoyed at school, for the way the names inspired dreams. Otherwise formal education wasn't making much impression on him. It was his older brother and sister who had the academic instinct. He was reasonable at art, but that was about it. He passed no exams. His mind, a mind that liked to play, was always running away from the prescribed subject. But in cycling he found something he wanted to learn about, something that engrossed him, something he could love.

There were a lot of reasons for this. The noise of thin tubular tyres on a descent, a smooth hiss thickened by the whirr of the wind in the spokes and the oiled hum

of hubs and gears. The beauty of the individual pieces of equipment, carefully machined from aluminium or steel and imported from Italy in boxes with the maker's name – Campagnolo – emblazoned on them in elegant script. A chainset, perhaps, or an alloy seat pillar – even now, almost 40 years later, he remembers the feeling of running his fingernail along the milled channel that ran down the back. A pair of Anquetil cycling shoes, with drilled soles, and white kid racing gloves, and a red leather track helmet that he bought in a cycling shop near Lake Como during his first trip abroad, aged 16. Going into the newsagent's shop to see if the special Tour de France magazine had arrived, and then turning the pages over and over again until they became dog-eared. Buying a tin of Evian merely because the mineral water company sponsored one of the Tour teams. Come to think of it, he still has that tin somewhere. And the magazines. And the helmet and the gloves and the racing shoes.

There were little tricks and habits to learn that indicated your membership of a brotherhood – but an inclusive one, whose only entry fee was commitment. Tricks such as taking your Brooks leather saddle off the bike and putting it in a vice and hammering the heads of the small brass rivets to flatten and enlarge

them (eventually the manufacturer spotted the fashion and started to make them that way). Habits like taking some sheets of brown paper with you when you raced so you could stuff them down the front of your shirt to keep the cold out on a descent, just like Anquetil or Coppi on the Alpe d'Huez. Or nerving yourself up to steal a plastic ice-cream sign from outside a shop on a ride one day and using it to wrap your folded spare tyre in, attaching it to the back of your saddle with the strap from a toeclip. Or being among the first to wear the club's new racing shirt, the one that wasn't made of heavy scratchy wool but of silk rayon, designed without food pockets at the front or back because that, just then, was the fashion. Cyclists were as obsessive about the details and the nuances as the people he would come to know later in his life, the ones who threaded red laces through their brown Hush Puppies, or spent decades searching for exactly the right kind of stone-coloured cotton raincoat.

But it wasn't just about the look and the style of the thing. On Saturday afternoons he raced. These were massed-start races on public roads, called criteriums. In those days there was no traffic control, just someone in a car going ahead to clear the way. Nowadays the riders drive to the races with their

more. His mind was too busy. It needed the noise and the chatter and the hectically changing order of a bunch of riders racing together, all watching each other and trying to read and respond to the emerging pattern.

equipment on the roof of their cars. In his time they cycled there and back, carrying their spare wheels on special clips, sometimes 60 or 70 miles each way.

He liked the massed-start races, the tactics and the strategy, the constant activity in the pack as riders attempted to break away and were caught. He got better at it, learning how to adjust his riding style for maximum efficiency, sitting back in the seat, holding the handlebars near the middle and using his arms for extra effort. Eventually he moved from the schoolboy to the junior category, which meant that he had to apply for a competition licence (he still has that somewhere, too). Track racing, on a banked concrete oval, didn't suit him so well. His best friend, who had big thighs and a strong back, beat him every time in the pursuits, where the riders started on opposite sides of the track, and the sprints, where everything went into an explosive final burst. His lanky frame might have been better suited to the lonely business of the time trials, in which you started at 30-second intervals and raced against the clock. But, all by himself on the road in the quiet of a Sunday morning, his mind would wander. The great time trialists could focus their thoughts on the very essence of what they were doing, and hold their concentration for an hour or

On Sundays there would be a club run, perhaps over Snake Pass, where the snow would lie thick in the winter and he could imagine himself to be on the Mont Ventoux, leading the Tour. Three nights a week he went out on a training run over a 38-mile circuit of the roads near his home, always the same route, sometimes with a club mate or two. At the furthest point, on a long and gruelling ascent far out in the country, which presented a particularly vicious test when the wind was from the east, he would pass a solitary oak tree set in a field, about 50 yards away from the road. He saw it through all the seasons, year after year. It became his tree, the symbol of his dedication.

All this was teaching him about himself and the world. He was learning that it isn't what you have but what you are, that if you've got a personality then people enjoy being with you, that if you've got humour it breaks down barriers. And he was learning about the

The Winner

value of teamwork, too; lots of interesting stuff about life, although he didn't realise it then.

At 15 he left school without a qualification to his name. When his father asked him what he wanted to do, the only thing he could think of was to say that he would like to be a professional racing cyclist. But he wasn't sure that he would be good enough, and there was no money in it in those days, so his father, who was a credit draper, spoke to a friend who ran a clothing warehouse. On Friday he left school and on Monday he started work.

He could cycle the four or five miles to the warehouse and back, every day, on his track bike. This had a low-geared fixed wheel, which meant that he had to keep his legs turning. He was certainly fit – he could pluck the skin off his thigh between his thumb and forefinger, like you would with the neck of a puppy, to show that there was no fat. That was what they did, he and his friends in the cycling club, to demonstrate their dedication to becoming more like their idols.

To begin with at the warehouse he was just the lad who fetched and carried, the youngest in the place by perhaps 20 years, but in time they gave him more and more responsibility until eventually he was becoming

involved in the buying side. Here, too, there were lessons to be picked up. This was an old-fashioned company, with a strong awareness of the importance of thrift in small matters. When no one was using a room, the lights would be switched off. They used the backs of old invoices for notepaper. When parcels arrived, the string and the wrapping paper would be carefully removed and used again. An old way of doing things, and about to become obsolete. But years later, when he found himself going round switching off lights in empty rooms, he knew where he had acquired the habit, and was grateful for it.

And then one day – afterwards he could never remember exactly when it was – he set off on a training run in his new rayon club shirt and his black-framed Buddy Holly sunglasses, and within five minutes his whole life would change.

✳

When he came out of hospital, three months later, the first thing he noticed was that the trees were green. So the accident must have happened in the winter, or maybe early spring. Anyway the sun had been shining, a low bright sun, straight into his eyes as he left home and cycled west along the suburban dual carriageway.

Photographs of Paul Smith by Harold Smith, Nottingham, 1950s.

The road was straight and he was turning a big gear, really motoring. He had his sunglasses on, and his head was down. Somehow, to judge by what happened next, the combination must have created a blind spot.

It was a red Austin A40, one of the little square-backed jobs designed in Italy by Pinin Farina, that he hit. The Austen was parked at the side of the road and he went straight into the back of it and flew over the top and landed on the bonnet and bounced back on to the road. When he tried to get up, the bottom half of his leg stayed on the ground. His femur was broken – even today he can still feel the place where it cracked – along with his nose, his collar bone and two fingers. There was blood everywhere.

He spent the next three months in the local hospital, in what had become known as the Ton Up Ward because it was where they took motorcyclists who came off their Triumph Bonnevilles or Norton Dominators out on the ring road on a Saturday night. And where miners from the local collieries were carried when a pitprop gave way and crushed them. There were eight deaths while he was in the ward, and the pain and screaming and evidence of mortality gave him another lesson in growing up.

In the first few weeks he was there his friends from the cycle club would come and visit, chatting away about their training runs and their races and their new bikes. It didn't cheer him up. In fact it upset him and he must have said something to his father because after a while they stopped coming and he no longer felt so depressed. He was getting fidgety, though. And humour was his way around that. He'd inherited it from his dad. Once on a run he'd said something that had made his friend Chris fall off his bike from laughing so much. Now the nurses called him the Praying Mantis because of his gangling limbs, and he got them laughing when he showed them how he had taught himself to eat his dessert with a spoon held between his toes.

He came home with a calliper on his leg and a pair of walking sticks, and just trying to stand up made him feel dizzy. He knew from the pain and the stiffness that he was never going to race again. For a while his life seemed a bit hazy, and in later years he could not recall whether it was during his time in hospital, or after he'd come out, that he met the person who took him to a pub in the city centre and introduced him to a different life. To life outside the camera club and the cycling club, in fact.

Jacques Anquetil, Tour de France celebrations, 1961 (photo: EMPICS), and racing in the Tour de France, 16 July 1962 (photo: Hulton Archive).

The pub was where the students from the art college went. Somehow he found himself among people who were talking about Mondrian and Warhol and Kokoschka and David Bailey, and listening to the Rolling Stones and Miles Davis and the Temptations, and he knew immediately that he wanted to be part of this world of colour and shapes and excitement. It was 1964, and he met an art student called Janet whose father had a bit of money and was willing to set her up in business. So he offered to help, and he found the premises and talked to estate agents and solicitors for the first time in his life. Before long they had a shop in an old two-storey building on the corner of a little street near the city centre, and he was running the men's department upstairs, ordering turtleneck sweaters and button-down shirts and stovepipe trousers. And because of that he never really felt the urge to mourn for his lost world of cycling.

Decades later he nevertheless found himself occasionally giving in to the impulse to buy a racing vest, sometimes even a bike. The gear levers and the sprocket sets and the dropped handlebars and the carefully cut lugs, where one frame tube joins another, still looked to him like things of beauty. And the modern riders were not so very far away, really, from

the men he had worshipped in his youth. On holiday in Italy one year he drove to a town to watch a big cycle race go through, and it came back to him how crazy it was to go all that way, when you knew that they'd be past and gone in a handful of seconds and you wouldn't know which rider was which or what position they were in. But he loved it, anyway, and sometimes when he was driving near his old home he would find himself on the lonely road with the long hard climb and he would see the oak tree, his tree, set back from the road and he would remember the dreams that might never have come true.

Louison Bobet (1925–1983), Tour de France champion, 1954
(photo: Hulton Archive).
Paul Smith with his Trek 'Y-bike' (Y22) at the Mud Dock Cycle Works
and Café, Bristol, 1996 (photo: Paul Box).

flair*

Statements by Paul Smith edited from previously published texts, articles or interviews, 1970–2001

al Street as seen from the window of Paul Smith's shop, 1980 (photographer unknown).

set up shop in Floral Street in 1979. In fact, I bought the original shop – the smaller of the two – in 1976, but by the time I got enough money together to pay for the property, to renovate and decorate, it was 1979. I think I was the first clothes shop here. Floral Street and James Street were completely empty, as were Bow Street and Russell Street. The market was closed. There weren't any fruiterers or greengrocers left. It was like a ghost town. After I opened it was very, very quiet for two years. Tumbleweed blowing in the streets – 'Is anyone out there?' Absolutely no one around. But we always chugged along. I had my wholesale business, too, and couldn't have survived without that. It is still my main business today. But as it happens the retail aspect in Covent Garden has been very significant indeed. 1978 to 1981 were difficult years. Nevertheless, then, as now, I didn't have a master plan. I own the business and I run it and I simply produce clothes.

I started as a fashion retailer and got into design because I couldn't find what I wanted to sell. So the two have always run parallel. Some points in my career were more centred around retail, and some around design. And I'm okay at design, I'm okay at business, but I'm really exceptional at neither. Now, because the Covent Garden shop is so popular and successful, retail has become a grown-up job – a serious job. In England, we're not allowed to be just a designer or just a retailer. So, the thing that got you there in the first place is the thing you're allowed to spend the least time doing. You have to be 90 per cent businessman and 10 per cent designer. Head cook and bottle-washer too – self-made people always find a problem with delegating.

We have a wealth of talent in England, a gold-mine of ideas, but we have an industry that doesn't know how to use these ideas. There is an industry for clothes, but not for fashion. My business is currently about 80 per cent export. The whole design problem in this country goes back to our history. Our priorities are just different from those of the French or the Italians, for example. Here, every guy's got a mortgage, a fridge, a colour TV. He likes his football, cricket and the pub. The same guy in Italy probably has a beaten up car and lives at home with his mother until he's well into his late twenties. He'll love food and clothes and has more money to spend on them both. Different priorities. The French and Italians tend to buy perhaps one piece a year. One per season. One good investment piece to be worn with a host of accessories – ties, shirts. So they'll buy a good suit. In most provincial towns here you don't even have a good clothes shop. General awareness of fashion design in Britain, though, is better than it was 20 years ago. What the world still needs, and what this country definitely needs, is a return to individualism, which the British have always been good at.

I'm not motivated by power or money.
What I am motivated by is a just a brilliant day, every day.

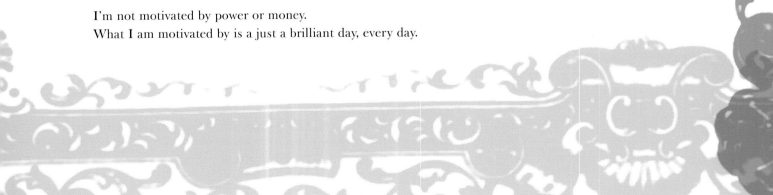

With 'Sigmund Freud' at 43 Floral Street, early 1980s.

I've had my own business since the age of 23 or 24. A lot of the reason we're still around is that I've always had my own shops. My job is to get somebody a jacket or a shirt. That's all it's about. So many designers surround themselves with subservience. They have chauffeur-driven cars, posh studios, and sadly they lose touch with what's going on around them, even in their own shops. There is nobody better at criticising or observing or talking to you about what you do than your customers.

This page and opposite: Floral Street

Paul's Filofax.

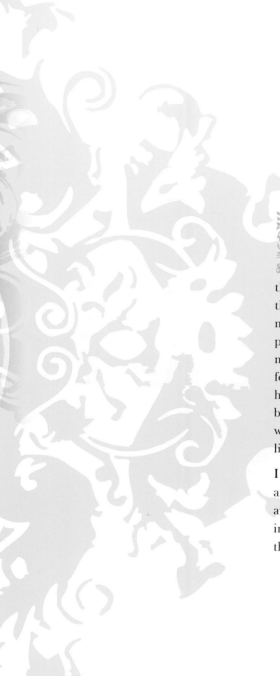

n 1979 I first went to the office of Norman & Hill, the original manufacturers of the Filofax, underneath a railway arch way over in the East End of London. It was a sad old company, run by just two people who didn't realise it had this wonderful, beautifully designed product. They offered to sell me the company, but somehow even at that time it didn't seem right to be manufacturing Filofaxes. I didn't mind selling them, but I didn't particularly want to own the whole kit and caboodle. Filofax eventually made a lot of money – a lot of it made by me – but I knew it wasn't for me. Our strength in the 1980s was learning to say no. We could have had licenses on just about anything, from cars to cigarette lighters, but I realised early on that I had to keep things just so, or else it wouldn't really be me. You've got to keep your sense of self or else there's little point in carrying on.

I was never comfortable with the whole idea of the grasping 1980s, and I think my background helped prevent me from getting carried away. Yes, I was the guy who found the Filofax, but all I did was introduce it to the world. Somebody else made it foul. I hated the greed, the corporate expansion, people going for it. All I did was let it roll.

ntil the mid-1980s, the hardest thing was justifying the name 'designer' for myself, when I only made such simple clothes. That was the hard one, to establish simplicity. I ended up designing clothes that I wanted to wear myself and felt good in. Well made, good quality, simple cut, interesting fabric, easy-to-wear. No-bullshit clothing. Luckily I found lots of other people who like the same thing.

In the 1970s I was asked so many times in interviews to define the Paul Smith look, and I never really managed to do it. Then, in 1981, when I was playing around with more traditional clothes, trying to reinvent the Prince of Wales check, I was asked this again and came up with 'classic with a twist', and it sort of stuck.

When I design a collection, I never ask for the opinions of anyone outside the fashion industry and, generally speaking, I don't ask the opinions of anyone except my assistant designers. I don't think that my designs influence the fashion on the street but, having said that, I don't think I take my inspiration from street fashion either. I'm sure most people relish the challenge of winning over a new audience. In my case, it would be people unfamiliar with the world of fashion I would want to win over – people who might think that designers are strange, egotistical people. In some cases, sadly, this is true.

26 January 1996 (photographer unknown).

Working in Floral Street, early 1980s.

am fascinated by the fact that whatever you pick up has been designed with a particular purpose in mind, whether it's grand or silly. This means that almost anything can serve as a visual prompt. A Chinese cigarette packet might suggest a new way to pack socks. A naff piece of fabric from a market in Egypt might make me think of a loud shirt that would look great under a cashmere suit. An Indian dancing doll, which someone has just plonked on a smart book, could spark an idea of juxtaposing kitsch with posh, rough with smooth, bright with bold, pattern on pattern.

I'd like to think that I've been fairly honest about what I do. I'm not selling a lifestyle or anything as crass as that. It's not even fashion, really, it's just clothes. I want my customers to put their own personality on what they buy, and the clothes to allow people to express their character rather than have it overwhelmed. I suppose my thing has always been about maximising Britishness. Paul Smith clothes have never had anything to do with class. In fact, they've always tried to subvert any of those connotations. I've made a point of mixing styles to such an extent that I hope they become classless, and street fashion has obviously helped in this regard – matt black with tat, and so on. The classes have always appropriated each other's clothing, whether knowingly or not, and I suppose I've exploited that to some extent. We've got the most extraordinarily creative people in this country, and the ingenuity of each new generation never ceases to amaze me. Other countries might have a larger quantity of better dressed people, yet they all look the same to me. We have a much more lateral way of thinking about everything, from the way we dress, to the music we make, to the things we consume. We're free spirited.

British men have had an uphill struggle with fashion. After the big bang of the early 1980s, I started pushing regular guys into fashionable clothes – a more colourful tie or sweater. I tried to make them feel it wasn't a problem – that it wasn't feminine. There was a time when if you walked into, say, a newspaper newsroom, with a colourful tie on, they'd jeer at you. I've always had a down-to-earth approach: if your skin gets dry, apply moisturiser – it's not a problem.

During the 1940s and 1950s, every man and child wore a suit. The only way to express yourself was how you wore it. In the 1960s – at the time of the early Stones and the Beatles, pre-hippie culture – I worked out how to put things together. This has been the basis of my look: taking essentially British items and customising them – adding unexpected details or colours. And then putting things together in different ways: a pinstripe suit with buttonholes in different colours, worn with a denim shirt and coloured shoes.

The wrong thing with the wrong thing is the speciality of the house here. Many designers have collections where, if you were to lay them out on the floor, you'd have lots of pieces which have to go together – you couldn't wear it unless you had the whole kit. If you take my collection, you can mix items with your own wardrobe, with your dad's trousers, or with another designer's clothes. It's about individuality.

I think human beings should be able to show their own characters: I don't want clothes to dominate. Lots of designer clothes are created to draw attention: 'Look at me. I'm fashionable, I'm rich, I'm part of the club.' That's fine if you're attention-seeking. But I want my clothes to say: 'Look at me, I am me'.

Eccentricity is an essential part of being British, so why shouldn't it be part of the business world? As for me, I have this feeling that I'm going to get even more eccentric as I get older.

Over the years so many designers who are better than me have come and gone. I think what I have, and they didn't have, was the ability to turn ideas into marketable ideas. I don't think I'm an exceptional designer. I think I've always been consistently good, which I feel is an achievement. I'd really just like to be remembered as a nice bloke.

So many young designers now become well known straight away, because of the way the media build them up. Nowadays, *Vogue*, *The Evening Standard*, *The Times*, *The Face* and others are all at the shows from the beginning, from graduate shows onwards. Designers aren't allowed to make their mistakes privately, like I did. Up in Nottingham, hidden away, nobody knew what the hell I was doing.

My first London shop was based on a minimal interior inspired by a love of the Bauhaus movement and Le Corbusier. The second shop, next door, was built in 1850 and had so much character, including amazing old floorboards, that I didn't have the heart to rip everything out. So the used, wooden-floored gentlemen's outfitters with a twist was born. I hate shops that are museums, or boxes. I like the smell of polish. I like the feeling that someone cares.

I always like my shops to be worth visiting. You never know quite what you are going to find – mad and wacky puppets hanging on the wall, vintage LPs, old *Beano* annuals or bound volumes of *Boys Own*, *Flair* or *Ambassador*, new and vintage photography books. On my travels to Japan, New York or Paris, I always like to put aside two hours to rush off to flea markets in search of interesting pieces. It all gets sent to my warehouse in Nottingham, and that's how I start building a collection of some kind. It makes a strong impact when it is all put in the stores.

Even back in 1979, in my first small space in Floral Street, I had a thin little cabinet with a glass top, that I had made especially to put things in, mostly from my holidays. I remember six interesting pen-knives from a hardware store, funny old pens and silly notebooks that were slightly kitsch. I put them in the shop just to make the shop more interesting. But the real difference came in 1982 when I started going to Japan, during the whole 1980s boom, for gadgets that were not available in Europe at all. I used to bring back 20 of this, 10 of that, fill my shop and they'd sell out in a week. It made me realise that people were starved of all that.

I have always been interested in how people trade. In my photographs you'll see some of the most amazing and resourceful innovations: a moustache salesman, a lady with a briefcase on her head selling T-shirts, a clothes shop in which your purchase is made through a hole in the ceiling. So I've always tried to keep my shops full of interest, where you can be 14 or 60, a student or a rock star. You can enjoy them. There's no obligation, they're friendly. There might be a bright red toothbrush next to a cashmere suit. You can come out having spent three quid or a thousand.

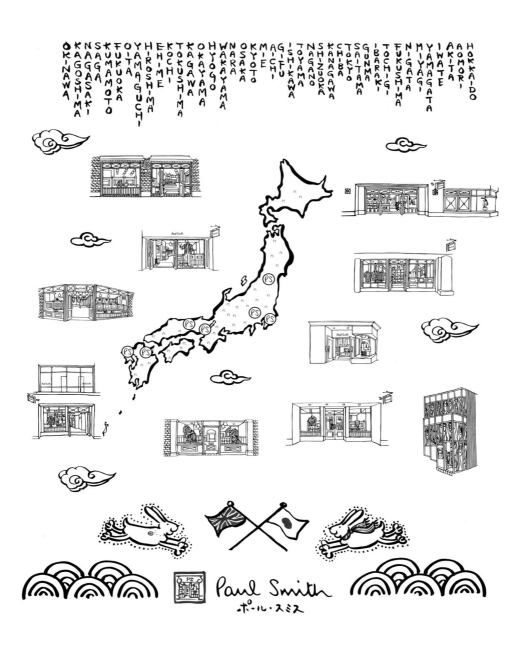

tokyo portfolio

"

The Japanese and the Italians are very, very conscious of design and its importance. They are probably no more professional as an industry than the British, but they are more intense and never complacent, especially the Japanese. It's very easy to think you've made it; I'm doing very well – my business has a turnover of about £315 million – but I don't consider that I can ease off. I'm still happy to work very hard because I love it and because in this game you have never made it. Fashion is about today and tomorrow. In Japan they are always searching for new avenues, they are always on the ball, always market-researching, always looking around the world, always aggressive and highly competitive. That's why business works so fantastically well in their country, despite the gloom since the 1990s. An important factor with the Italians, too, is that they have a lot of natural style. They also have a very good relationship with the Government, regarding promotion and the importance of the fashion trade.

What I learned from my father's sense of humour was one of the main reasons, in my opinion, why my business is so big in Japan. He'd hide behind the door and pretend someone was grabbing his head, or something, and play jokes all the time. But very visual. I remember in those early days in Japan, being at a meeting or at a table for dinner with my new business partners and maybe only one person spoke a little bit of English. In situations like that, visual stuff comes into play and would help to create a feeling of comradeship. You know, there'd be a really serious meeting, then I'd fumble around in my briefcase and pull out a rubber chicken. Everyone would curl up with laughter.

So many people have the wrong idea about Japan. When I give any kind of talk, the first thing businessmen want to know is: 'How do I get into Japan?' And the answer is, you go there to learn, to enjoy it, to get a feel for the place. You don't go there just to make money. A lot of important designers are not at all successful in Japan, and they don't deserve to be. They don't understand that the Japanese are an incredibly charitable people, and if they see that you're willing to let your hair down a bit, they love you even more. You've got to believe in them as much as you believe in yourself.

In the beginning, I just loved it so much in Japan, and I really wanted my business to work there. Back then, in the early 1980s, you hardly saw any 'gajin'. People stared because I was tall. I used to travel around a lot. Much more than I can now. I'd walk, and walk, and walk. I would often be the only foreigner on a train – people would come and try their English on me.

To succeed in Japan, or anywhere, you need a good balance of new ideas, commercial sense, and a general awareness. And great business partners, which I'm lucky enough to have. That, and to be able to think quickly. I aim to run a down-to-earth company that has a heart, and the Japanese liked that and gave me many generous opportunities. Having good luck helps too, of course, but recognising and taking opportunities is the key.

"

This page: signing a T-shirt and posing as a window display in the Paul Smith shop , Shibuya, Tokyo (photos: Lance Martins).
(illustration overleaf by Studio Omame, Tokyo; www.studioomame.com)

Paul Smith shop in the Shibuya area of
Tokyo, with window display and mannequins
by Kacchi (photos: Kacchi).

I have more than 240 shops and a £212 million retail business in Japan. I have worked hard at it: as of Spring 2001 I have been there 52 times and met the people and the press. Rather than catwalk shows, twice a year in Tokyo I have what are called 'tenjikai', which are separate 'exhibitions' of new collections, ranging from accessories to the mainline collections for men and women. I talk to the staff and involve myself in absolutely every side of the Paul Smith business in Japan – even the interior shop design and the cups and saucers. Many people in the greedy 1980s were invited to Japan and said, 'I am a designer. Sign here. Thank you, we will send you a few drawings every now and again.' Ten years on they still wonder why they do not have a decent business there. It is simply because they have never made the necessary effort. Fashion is not about yesterday. You cannot rely on your history very long. If you are not 100 per cent involved, you might as well pack it in. It is a carousel, constantly going round: you do Spring, Winter, Spring again – if you want to be in the game, you have to do it properly.

Paul Smith Women Tenjikai, Tokyo, April 2000 (photos: Robert Violette).

In the early 1980s I had a small show in the British Embassy in Paris based on a salon atmosphere, which was right for the time. The clothes were simple classics, usually with an unexpected extra detail, but nothing outlandish. It is the way things are put together that makes the difference, in Japan too. People then had money and ate out a lot. They all had nice cars, the dreaded carphone – and also everybody wanted to look chic. Everybody had a Visa card. They all really wanted to show that they were important. Young people were willing to wear suits and were not embarrassed about saying that they had money. That was what the 1980s were all about and my clothes reflected the times, but now and again we had a shot of nonsense. I bought some seeds for my garden at my house in Italy, photographed the packet and made a shirt from the print.

A survey in the 1990s by a Japanese market research company said that 55 per cent of the creative ideas in the world now come from Britain. When it comes to manufacturing those ideas, though, only 3 per cent of them were actually made in Britain. The creative ideas coming out of Japan amounted to only 3 per cent of the world market, yet 55 per cent of those were made in Japan itself. For example, Casio of Japan came over to hire the young British design team Seymour Powell, because they wanted a British designer for their watches.

Another example is the Skorpion motorbike, launched in March 1993 and also designed by Seymour Powell. In the early 1960s Britain had the finest motorbike industry in the world. Then something called 'complacency' set in; we thought we were the best and so we did not do our market research, check things out or 'think global and act local'. Honda, Suzuki and all the big Japanese companies came along; the result was that we lost our motorbike industry.

Then there is the insulin pen. Before it was invented, diabetics had to use needles to inject themselves with insulin. This pen, which can work in your pocket, avoiding the embarrassment of injecting, won a BBC Design Award. It is a brilliant idea, designed by an Englishman. It was offered to Glaxo, who would not pay the development costs, so the design went to a Danish company, who quickly sold three million of the pens.

Paul Smith shops in Tokyo, anti-clockwise from top: Shibuya shop and offices of Paul Smith; women's shop; new Red Ear shop.

Entrance to, and creative meeting at, Paul Smith Men Tenjikai, Tokyo, April 2000 (photos: Robert Violette).

Another British design that started abroad is a new type of vacuum cleaner, designed by someone from the Royal College of Art. He made it in his workshop in Bath, and it took four years to develop. He tried for many years to involve a British company in the manufacture of his cleaner, but nobody was interested. He took it to Japan and after six weeks he was signed up. By the early 1990s they had already sold many millions worth of his cleaner.

He then brought it back to England, and tried to get the Welsh Development Board to set him up with a factory, to create jobs. They were not interested, so he had to set up a factory on his own. Here is a designer who has had to set up a factory to manufacture his own product! I am glad to say he is doing very well, even today. His name is James Dyson.

With security guard outside the Paul Smith
Tenjikai, TFT building, Tokyo, April 2000
(photo: Katsu).

"

In the beginning when I started to work
with manufacturers, I tried to communicate
exactly what it is that I want – not just
saying that I want a good quality shirt, but
being specific, down to cuff size, exactly the
right buttons and so on. Also, it's important
to use people for what they are good at.
I found a factory making only football
scarves and standard grey V-neck school
pullovers. Over a period of time I got them
to make the same style that they felt
comfortable making, but in more exciting
colours. I ended up taking the knitwear
mechanic to the pub, and he gradually
became enthused with the ideas I put
forward, so we were able to add stripes,
and slowly but surely we ended up with
really stylish sweaters.

Doing business in Japan is the same. It
means trying to see things through their
eyes. Over the years I have built up a
respect for and understanding of their ways,
and this has certainly helped my business
there to succeed. I'm enormously fond of
Japan and my Japanese colleagues. That
helps a lot too.

"

Taxi doors that open automatically.

No tipping anywhere – service included.

Plastic food in restaurant windows to help you pick a dish.

Ashtrays for pedestrians on stands at traffic lights, even though I'm a non-smoker.

A little piece of home – my shops in Kobe, Kyoto and Tokyo, decorated with English shop fittings.

my top five things from Japan

At Bunkaya Zen, one of Paul Smith's favourite shops in Tokyo (photos: Robert Violette).

true brit

jim davies

'Paul Smith: True Brit' was an exhibition not so much about fashion, as the process of design. Through the life and work of Britain's leading designer of menswear, it demonstrated that inspiration is all around us, that humble, everyday objects can often provide clues for potent visual ideas. This exhibition also examined the often overlooked craft aspect of fashion: the importance of tailoring skills, fabric selection and attention to detail. Finally, and perhaps most importantly, it reminded us that even in a context of relative formality, clothes can always be liberating and fun.' – Jim Davies

This text by Jim Davies was first published in the Japanese catalogue for the exhibition 'Paul Smith: True Brit', originated and supervised by The Design Museum, London. The exhibition was first shown at The Design Museum from 5 October 1995 to 10 April 1996 and then toured Japan at the Mitsukoshi Museum of Art, Tokyo (18 September to 11 October 1998), the Kobe Fashion Museum, Kobe (17 October to 27 December 1998), and the IMS Hall, Fukuoka (3 January to 24 January 1999). No alterations to the present-tense original text have been made. Some updated figures are given in brackets.

who is paul smith?

'A mangled bike is probably a strange thing
to kick off an exhibition with.' – paul smith

Strange perhaps, but highly symbolic. The rusty, buckled bike is a salutary reminder that as a 17-year-old, cycling-mad Paul Smith was fortunate to emerge alive from a horrific road accident. A collision with a parked car left him in traction in a Nottingham hospital for three months and recuperating for six. It also represents a pivotal moment in the designer's life, one which saw him switch his allegiance from cycling to fashion. Within 20 or so years of the crash, Smith had established himself as the preeminent designer of menswear in Britain. Today [1998] there are eight Paul Smith shops in London [2001: 11], his original Nottingham shop, another in Manchester, one each in New York and Paris, five in Hong Kong, two in Singapore, four in Taiwan, one in Manila, plus an astounding 200 outlets in Japan [2001: 240]. He is the biggest-selling European designer in the East, outselling the likes of Armani, Gucci and Chanel.

That he has managed to maintain and consolidate his position in such a notoriously fickle industry is as much a measure of his business nous as his creative instincts. Smith appears to have an uncanny ability to anticipate, and even spark off, trends not only in fashion but in the wider context of popular culture – he was responsible for popularising the Filofax, boxer shorts and the eight-button polo shirt, for example. But it is Smith's intuitive take on design which has laid the foundations for his lasting success. He famously defined the Paul Smith look as 'classic with a twist'; a combination of quality and quirkiness, wearability and wit. The principles of traditional craftsmanship and tailoring are retained, but given a contemporary edge; classic styles and materials are deconstructed and recontextualised.

He is one of the few working designers who manages to transmit a genuine sense of fun and mischief, which lends character and humanity to his collections. 'I've always tried to design clothes which allow the person to be an individual, rather than making them look like part of a high fashion gang,' explains Smith. 'Having said that, I make a point of trying to appeal to a certain type of person – a person of free will and free spirit, a little like myself.'

cycle shirts

'Between the ages of 11 and 17, I had nothing else in my life, apart from cycling.'

His dreams of becoming a pro cyclist shattered, Paul Smith began frequenting an infamous Nottingham pub called the Bell Inn, where he quickly fell in with a crowd of art students, including his partner and life-long inspiration Pauline Denyer.

Pauline had previously studied fashion at the Royal College of Art, and had moved up to Nottingham to teach. 'I was becoming fascinated with life in a way I had never experienced it,' he recalls. 'Art, architecture, fashion, music, all these things suddenly came into my orbit and I loved it.'

It's telling that fashion is third on the list; Smith's interests and reference points have always extended well beyond the confines of his craft, which bring a freshness and sense of the unexpected to his approach. Smith's collection of cycling T-shirts, framed early photographs and school reports, are a visual representation of his boy racer days, when he regularly put in around 350 miles training a week, pedalling furiously from Nottingham to Coventry, Derby or Sheffield — and back. 'I would go to bed early and eat sensibly. I took cycling really seriously, but in reality I don't think I ever believed I could

make a career out of it. Fashion is a lot safer.' Smith remains a keen — though less obsessive — cyclist. On occasion a nod to the distinctive lines of close-fitting, striped cycling gear may even surface in one of his collections.

With the benefit of hindsight, his school reports make fascinating reading; was Smith's headmaster, Mr Roberts, a part-time psychic? 'It has been a pleasure to have this lad (Paul Brierly Smith) at school. He has developed and should do well at whatever post he secures.'

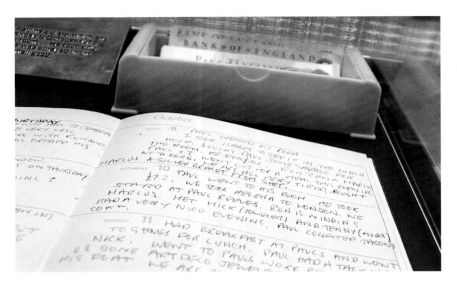

union jack

'I have always been interested in maximising Britishness.'

The Union Jack, or Union flag, was first introduced in 1603 to symbolise the union of the crowns of England and Scotland. It's basically an amalgam of the cross of St George and the diagonal cross of St Andrew. The cross of St Patrick was added in 1801, when the parliaments of Great Britain and Ireland were united. The distinctive patchwork of red, white and blue is laden with history and meaning, evoking different emotions and connotations for different generations. In the 1960s, it was hijacked by the emerging youth movement, and came to epitomise the 'swinging sixties' of Carnaby Street and the Beatles. The Mods used it to brighten up their drab parkas, and it was later adapted in a more sinister fashion by skinheads and punks. Since then, it has emerged regularly as a fashion motif, its meaning and application in a constant state of flux.

The potency of the Union Jack wasn't lost on Paul Smith either; some of his first silk-screen T-shirt and handkerchief designs were based on the flag, and he has continued to play with its constituent parts, changing its colour and context in numerous designs. Smith, who takes conspicuous pride in his origins, has transformed his quirky idea of Britishness into an international language of fashion: 'Other countries might have a larger quantity of better dressed people, yet they all look the same to me,' he says. 'The British have a much more lateral way of thinking about everything, from the way we dress to the music we make, to the things we consume. … We're free spirited.'

the first shop

'We didn't even call it a shop – we called it a room.'

On 9 October 1970, armed with £600 savings, Paul Smith opened his very first shop. It was called Paul Smith Vêtement Pour Homme and located at 6 Byard Lane, down a tiny back alley in the centre of Nottingham. The weekly rent was just 50p.

The 12-foot square metal frame featured in 'Paul Smith: True Brit' gives an idea of the size of the premises (compact to say the least), and various artefacts – the original till with the first day's takings, Pauline's diary, and a selection of photographs – build up an impression of the place.

The bottle of Eau Sauvage aftershave in the glass cabinet is a little more obscure: this was to disguise the smell of Paul's faithful Afghan hound, Homer, which tended to dominate the windowless room. Vêtement was originally open only on Fridays and Saturdays; Smith having to work during the week selling fabrics, making up suits for wholesalers and window dressing, and later working as a stylist and consultant, to bring in some more steady money. But soon the shop was buzzing. It was the only outlet outside London which stocked Margaret Howell and Kenzo, and after a while, slowly but surely, Pauline and Paul began introducing their own designs on to the racks.

evolution

'How big can we grow? I don't think
we've scratched the surface yet.'

It couldn't have taken long to count the takings after the first day's trading at Vêtement, Paul Smith's original Nottingham shop. They came to a modest £52. Today [1998], it's quite a different story. Smith heads up an impressive international fashion empire of nearly 250 shops and eight clothing collections. An extraordinary new flagship store, Westbourne House, has opened in London's Notting Hill. Annual turnover of wholesale, retail and licensed business is valued at £171 million [2001: £315m]. Two thirds of the business is export, placing the company in the higher echelons of international fashion and netting Smith the prestigious Queen's Award for Export in 1995 [and a knighthood in 2000].

Despite the steady expansion, Paul Smith himself remains deeply involved in the day-to-day running of the firm. He is the company's chairman as well as its frontline designer, and his infectious enthusiasm and energy permeates every aspect of the business. And even now you might catch him on the shop floor in one of his many shops serving a customer. Smith has attempted to replicate faithfully the ambience of his first London store in Floral Street in his various outlets throughout the world – right down to the unmistakable smell of wax polish. Antique mahogany counters, oak floors and dark glass cabinets housing all manner of curios and accessories create a relaxed, if somewhat unlikely setting for some of the more extravagant lines of clothing. Some interiors have been transported in their entirety from the UK. The Kobe shop in Japan was originally a chemist's shop in Sheffield, the Tokyo shop a chocolate seller's from Newcastle.

organisation

'The conveyor belt is a
childlike way of showing
what I do for a living.'

When you walk out of a Paul Smith shop
proudly clutching your carrier bag, you're
more likely to be wondering where to have
lunch than how the contents actually arrived
there. One thing's for certain: your just
purchased garment will have made a long
and tortuous journey. The complete cycle,
from original idea to finished article, requires
rigorous planning and organisation and
typically takes several months.

A zany, 32-foot model created by the artist
Ian Bilbey depicts the various stages in the
development of an article of Paul Smith
clothing, its progress charted using an
ingenious miniature conveyor belt and a
collection of comical plastic figurines.

Ian Bilbey has worked with Paul Smith for
a number of years, conceiving fantastical
abstract window displays for the Floral Street
shops and a series of one-off pieces including
cufflinks, miniature painted cows and
elaborately painted shoe soles.

Here, vague ideas and conceptual thoughts are turned into practical reality; the physical component of pattern-cutting and the making-up of garment samples follows; then suddenly we're in Paris for a make-or-break fashion show.

The publicity campaign is up next, followed by full-scale production; the new collection is distributed to Paul Smith's network of shops, and finally the 'happy customer' emerges. That's you, clutching your carrier bag, by the way.

Most of the production process still takes place in an unassuming warehouse on the outskirts of Nottingham.

brochures

'We've moved from classical photography to kitsch bad taste and back again.'

Orchestrated by the London-based design company Aboud•Sodano, Paul Smith's award-winning publicity material has evolved and developed in tandem with his fashion collections. Brochures are characterised by clean, unfussy art direction and a lateral, imaginative slant on what can often be a formulaic medium.

In the early 1990s, Paul Smith brochures and ads championed the use of 'real people', usually friends or friends of friends of the designers, who were photographed reportage style by Hugh Hales-Took on Lundy, a small Island off the west coast of England. Typically, six or so young men are shown clowning around among the sculptural rock formations and windswept beaches of the island, dressed in Paul Smith clothing, which was made even more striking by the unexpected setting.

Rival companies soon cottoned on to the approach, so Paul Smith moved on. In 1993, a brochure showcasing a sixties-inspired collection used a series of stark head-and-shoulder portraits by David Bailey, who at the time had more or less dropped out of photography to concentrate on a career in commercials direction. Again, the models were mostly unknowns, though later publications introduced the odd celebrity, including the actor John Hurt and the advertising guru John Hegarty. Suddenly Bailey was resurgent; in demand by a host of fashion magazines including *Vogue*, *Arena* and *Harper's Bazaar*. The next batch of publicity material was the most radical of all, using tacky cover illustrations from Mills and Boon romance novels, and subsequently bright cartoonesque drawings of Paul Smith clothes with heavy, exaggerated black outlines. More recently, Paul Smith brochures have adopted a hardcore fashion feel, featuring blurred, enigmatic colour photography by photographer Mario Testino.

Brochures for Paul Smith's workwear label, R. Newbold, meanwhile, allow Aboud•Sodano to cut loose and experiment with different formats. One took the form of series of giant rolled-up posters in a tube; another mimicked a record sleeve, with the disc-shaped inserts inside bearing strange words and abstract imagery; another, for R. Newbold's range of stormwear, was printed on waterproof plastic and used dramatic shots of soaking models.

craftsmanship

'Not everything has to be mass produced, you know.'

There are all sorts of reasons for Paul Smith's achievements – his personality, his flair, his aptitude for business. But the care and attention lavished on each item of clothing that leaves the shop underpins his success. When you buy a Paul Smith suit or shirt, you know it's well made. Quality control is uncompromising. 'I'm a big fan of established British craftsmanship, and it's something I've tried to emulate in my work,' says Smith. His father was a draper, and Smith himself used to carry garments around a warehouse in Nottingham's lace district when he left school aged 15. His respect for the craft and heritage of his line of work is extremely deep-rooted.

The exhibition offers a peek into the arcane world of traditional British tailoring, showing a bank of paper patterns, a suit at five different stages of construction and a pair of shoes at various stages before completion. Often these items will be hand-finished, some by Smith himself. Attention to detail and stringent standards set the designer's work apart from many of his competitors; as his business expands he is determined to maintain his reputation for high-quality, immaculately finished clothing.

window displays

'Good shop window displays are a mixture of theatre and visual advertising.'

In effect, shop-window displays are a 24-hours-a-day, 365-days-a-year advertisement – a kind of dynamic 3D poster. For Paul Smith, they represent yet another opportunity to project his highly particular visual sensibility. Though the structure, theme and content of the displays vary greatly, they all tend to share a sense of humour and quirky dramatic intrigue.

The key to their impact is undoubtedly the fact that they are changed every week to ten days, compared to the typical four to eight weeks for most shops. This means they are always fresh and surprising, even to regular passers-by. Often, visual jokes or plays on words are incorporated into

the tableaux by using simple props from hardware stores or joke shops to interact with the clothes and accessories on display. Recently, the double window of Paul Smith's Floral Street shop featured a selection of belts stuck to the glass by their buckles. In the other window, several large magnets were attached to the glass, giving the impression that they were actually holding the suspended belts in position.

The displays deliberately look as if they were cobbled together quickly, lending a certain spontaneity and 'personal' touch – as if Smith had created them himself. They are simple, highly focused and fun. Slapstick looms large – it's immediate

and overblown, perfect for making people stop in their tracks. But the finer details must not be overlooked either: creased or badly fitting clothing can easily ruin a display. London takes the lead in generating most of the ideas for Paul Smith window displays. Photographs and display reports are sent to shops all over the world, but only as a source of guidance and inspiration – conformity is a no-no.

words not pictures

'I always carry a small note-book to jot down ideas –
I've got through hundreds.'

It's evident from the volume of paraphernalia on display in this exhibition that Paul Smith is an inveterate hoarder. But, interestingly, he collects thoughts as well as objects. Smith is constantly scribbling into one of his orange Rhodia notebooks, recording observations or passing fancies, inconsequential musings, colour combinations, lists of words which mean nothing to anyone but himself. For a fashion designer, it's perhaps curious that he doesn't draw – he puts this down to his lack of formal training. On the rare occasions he does attempt to sketch, the results are a child-like muddle of dots and ticks, which bear little resemblance to a finished design. Ultimately, these doodles serve their purpose as aides-mémoire, and their of lack of finesse is endearing in a man as outwardly sophisticated as Smith. Some of the hurried scribblings may eventually find their way into a collection as an idea for a cut of trouser, perhaps, or a print or a shirt –

or they may be discarded altogether. Sculptor Richard Wentworth has created an installation of some of Smith's many notebooks, interspersed with mounted magnifying glasses which pick up haphazard phrases and doodles, mirroring the random nature of Smith's creative thought processes. 'Every thought could come in handy,' says Smith. 'It might turn out to be rubbish, but you won't know unless you write it down.'

balance

'I've made a point of
mixing styles so that
they become classless.'

Paul Smith's designs rely on achieving a critical balance. Between formality and eccentricity; exuberance and sobriety; traditional and contemporary. A narrow corridor in 'Paul Smith: True Brit' illustrates this facet of his work, lining a row of restrained dark blue and black suits against one wall, opposite a series of yellow, orange and bright green suits on the other.

Both ranges start with examples of menswear and move almost organically into womenswear. It's tempting to pigeonhole – one wall represents the more formal, classical side of Paul Smith, the other the playful, expressive part – but that would miss the point. Some of the dark suits exhibit the characteristic quirky touches that Smith has become known for; while many of the brights are made from tweed, a highly traditional material, but deployed here in a variety of unusual shades and colours.

black is black?

The classic suit is one of the most challenging items for a men's fashion designer, but it has become something of a Paul Smith speciality. Though the parameters are tightly defined, it's still an easy thing to do badly. And if you also strive – as Smith does year in, year out – to bring something a little different to the equation, you're potentially in even deeper water. Extraneous details, such as zips, buckles and decorative accessories, have a tendency to destroy the integrity of a suit; but there are more fundamental ways to alter the tone and feel of such an archetypal design.

The 'Black is Black' section of 'Paul Smith: True Brit' graphically demonstrates the importance of choice of fabric. Six identically cut black suits are hung side by side on a plain white wall. They comprise a 118 jacket (three-button, single-breasted, longer length jacket with two vents at the back) and a 11T trouser (flat fronted, slim leg). But each suit has been made up from a different type of material, which completely changes its character – from the way it hangs to its look and texture.

Visitors are invited to feel a selection of material swatches positioned in front of the six suits and then touch the suits themselves to fully appreciate the implications of switching materials. 'Young designers have a tendency to over design,' says Smith. 'I'm just trying to show that it's best to keep things simple, but that you can still say something.'

observation

'Literally anything can spark off an idea.'

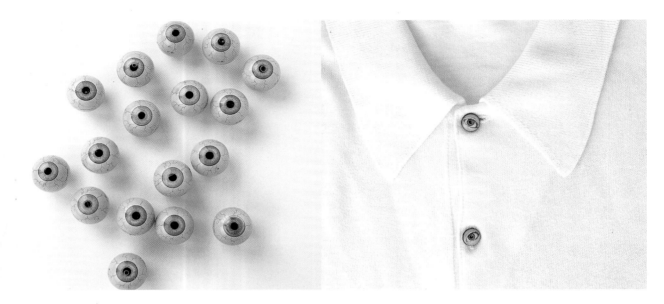

The underlying premise of 'Paul Smith: True Brit' is that there is the potential for inspiration in virtually everything around you. Visual clues and prompts — objects, books, photographs — are the most obvious sources of ideas for designers, but even an energising piece of music or an evocative smell might just do the trick. A heightened sense of awareness and an ability successfully to translate observations into workable design ideas has always been one of Paul Smith's strengths. 'You can find inspiration in everything,' he believes. 'If you can't find it, then you're not looking properly'

Smith's trademark photo-print shirts are probably the most obvious manifestation of his belief; in the past he's used clouds, budgies, plastic spaghetti, a Kandinsky painting, seed packets, a pile of oranges and a Tuscan woodpile as wild all-over shirt patterning. He's also plundered Mod iconography for a series of T-shirts and show invites, while some of his favourite strip cartoons have found their way into jacket shapes and trouser lengths.

Smith has a passion for vernacular or 'found' design, odd artefacts which are so much a part of everyday life that we barely notice them any more; take them out of their normal context, however, and they suddenly become visible and intriguing. As well as his notebooks, he is rarely without a camera; and, of course, his extensive travels provide him with a wealth of visual stimuli.

collections

'People can see how my work has changed –
I was going to say progressed – over the years.'

Fashion shows are audacious pieces of theatre, in which top international designers project a flavour of their forthcoming collections. In their attempts to impress the world's buyers and fashion press, they have become ever more extreme and extravagant events, exploiting obscure obtuse staging and ever-louder hardcore music.

One of Paul Smith's first breakthroughs in this area was in 1978 in a concrete modernist art gallery in Les Halles, Paris. He sent black models down the runway in a wild assortment of silks in turquoise, raspberry and yellow, as thumping dub reggae juddered the chairs of the assembled throng.

'You have between 20 and 25 minutes to show the world what you have to offer and it costs from £60,000 to £100,000 to put on. For me a fashion show is like a moving shop window,' says Smith. 'And since your shop window is your most important asset, you should exploit it as best you can.'

paul's office

'People are always amazed by the mad things I have in my room.'

A Paul Smith suit may be a masterpiece of elegant understatement, but a Paul Smith office most certainly isn't. The man is a compulsive collector of … well, just about any kitsch or curious object he can lay his hands on. His office, situated above the immaculate Floral Street shop with its carefully folded sweaters and perfectly hung suits, resembles a ramshackle curiosity shop more than a quiet haven in which the designer can collect his thoughts and catch up on paperwork. It is piled high with 1950s and 1960s magazines, antique cameras, water pistols, comic book annuals, strangely shaped buttons, toy rabbits, penknives and footballs. There are literally boxes and boxes of the stuff; he just can't help himself. 'It's quite childish, I suppose,' he says, without a hint of embarrassment.

Smith's fondness for tin robots of all shapes and sizes and antique bakelite radios is well known; some of these gizmos have even been known to spill over into his shops. His predilection for velvet Elvis paintings and rubber chickens is something he generally keeps to himself, however.

'If I see something strange or funny, or something I've not seen before, I want it,' he explains. 'I've always been fascinated with how people solve design problems, and most of the things in my office have been designed with a particular purpose in mind, whether it's a grand purpose or a silly one. A pencil, a Chinese cigarette packet, a wristwatch, a robot. Any of these things could spark off an idea for a T-shirt or a way to pack socks, whatever. Also, you'd be surprised how many people send me things — strange things, weird things.'

Again, this magpie mentality is borne out of Smith's unshakeable belief that inspiration can emanate from the most unexpected of quarters. He surrounds himself with bizarre, whimsical objects just in case they can provide a vital signpost to his next big idea. For the exhibition, Smith's office has been recreated using many of its actual contents. 'It's a bit worrying,' he says. 'I had a big clear-out for the exhibition, but the place has already filled up again.'

Oddly enough the Mini, which came to epitomise the spirit of 1960s Britain – and famously starred alongside Michael Caine and Noel Coward in the cult caper movie 'The Italian Job' – was dreamed up by a Turkish-born designer working for Austin Morris. The man in question was Sir Alec Issigonis, whose revolutionary concept car was launched in the UK back in 1959. With its low centre of gravity and amazing power to weight ratio, it introduced the excitement of front-wheel drive, high speed and agility to the mass market for the first time. Someone from Rover, which currently manufactures the Mini car, spotted a particular item in Paul Smith's Spring/Summer 1995 Womanswear collection, which suggested an idea. The show was based on a terrible pun, featuring a bold black-and-white print of a Mini car on a 'mini' skirt. From this, the Rover person correctly deduced that Smith had a soft spot for the Mini, and duly commissioned him to design a limited-edition model. The result was Paul Smith through and through.

The interior is black leather and the coachwork is a discreet blue, based on the colour of one of Smith's own shirts. He simply handed over a small square of material and asked for the colour to be matched. Launching the car in Tokyo in April 1998, he theatrically pulled his shirt out of his trousers to reveal a neat, square hole in the shirt-tail.

There is the inevitable twist. Open the glove compartment, boot or the bonnet and you'll be dazzled by a vivid citrus green – reminiscent of the luminous linings of one of Smith's otherwise sober suits. There are other neat touches too: foglamps (so British); enamelled gold-plated badges on the bonnet; and the name on the old-style instrument gauges, made by a company called 'Smith', has been cleverly changed to 'Paul Smith'.

For 'Paul Smith: True Brit', Smith has conceived another, one-off Mini. This time, he's been a little more extravagant; it's painted in ultra-bright candy stripes based on the patterning of one of his more expressive shirts.

paul smith mini

'The designer of the Mini must be a genius.
It looks better and better every year and is still
driving like a dream.'

the things they say
about paul smith*

'We have always described our projects as "keeping plates spinning". I can just about deal with two, with a look of grim determination. Paul, however, can spin innumerable plates with a grace and humour that puts me to shame. Has he ever dropped a spinning plate? No. But he has, on rare occasions, disposed of one, usually due to mistrust. Then the side of Paul that people rarely see is exposed.'

Pauline Denyer

'The man maketh the clothes – genius, gentleman, Paul Smith.'

Hanif Kureishi, author, playwright, director

'It seems that the Japanese are fascinated by the cultural icons of Northern England. One enlightened denizen of Kyoto recently informed me, "We here are in awe of your three great national treasures: the Brontes, fustian, and, of course, Paul Smith." Now if that isn't the ultimate accolade, I'll eat my Stetson. With extra wasabi.'

Glen Baxter, illustrator

'I haven't got much time for most of the younger designers, but Paul Smith's OK. He understands the four-button jacket.'

Sir Hardy Amies, couturier

'What do businessmen see in this no-nonsense designer with a name that is a byword in England for Mr. Ordinary? Maybe, as he strides in, they catch a glimpse of the sunshine orange silk lining to the plain grey suit.'

Suzy Menkies, Fashion Editor,
International Herald Tribune

'The ultimate multifaceted comedian of fashion design. Or is that chameleon?'

Tom Dixon, furniture designer

'Paul has a great eye for finding amusing or beautiful things in unexpected places, and for spotting the little things. He loves to share what he finds. It's what makes him not just a great designer, but unfailingly good company. He persuaded me to go to Japan when it was still as exotic as Mars. He took me to see a gallery in the East End, flooded with black engine oil, before Charles Saatchi bought it. And he sent me a sack full of new socks to replace the holed specimens I'd disgraced myself with in the "shoes-off" restaurants of Tokyo.'

Deyan Sudjic, Editor, *Domus*

'I've only ever bought a pair of boots from the man. But they're bloody great boots.'

Vic Reeves, comedian, cheese aficionado

'I've known him for 17 years and he hasn't changed. Not one bit. He's an extraordinary man who, despite his profound success, has managed to hold on to the very things that most people lose within a year of being in the fashion business: enthusiasm. He has a child-like (and I don't mean childish) view of the world. He is grateful for his life. I once asked him if he ever got depressed. He looked at me as if I was an alien. "Shit, no," he said. "I wake up in the morning and think, what shall I do with today?" He never bullshits and he isn't afraid of expressing his feelings. If he likes something, he says so. If he doesn't, he says that too. If this government had any sense, they'd make him the Minister for Getting Things Done. If every British company had Paul Smith at the head of it, we'd be away.'

Sally Brampton, author and journalist

'The name's made up, of course. I'm actually one of the Von Heidelbergs.'

Sir Paul Smith

*From *Paul Smith: True Brit* (exhibition catalogue, ed. Dylan Jones), The Design Museum, London, 1995, pp. 62–75.

paul smith photographs

Photography has always interested me. I suppose I could have become a photographer, had I not gone down the route that ended up in fashion. It's not anything I considered seriously. I started taking photographs when I was about 11 years old, I think. Photography was familiar to me, because my father had a darkroom in the attic of our house. His Rolleiflex was always lying around. On Tuesday nights I sometimes went to the Beeston Camera Club with him, where my dad was a founder member. And sometimes I went with him to their lectures, but I'd get fidgety – they could be quite dull. One of the most impressive ones, though, was about Cartier-Bresson. That in particular had a great impact on me, in terms of understanding the power of 'caught moments' or ad-lib shots.

Many of my friends are photographers: David Bailey, Mario Testino, Albert Watson; I own quite a nice collection of vintage cameras, and of photographs by Horst, Parkinson, Weber and others. At one time, briefly, I did do a bit of photography for magazines like *The Face* and *Arena*, but I soon realised that it was an embarrassment. I wasn't really good enough. If you saw my collection of snaps, which number in the thousands, there are shots where you might think, 'What the hell was that?!' The answer would most certainly be: *It should have been a nice shot, but I was driving along in a car and I didn't get quite enough time to roll the window down!* Nearly all my snaps are spontaneous – and I use just any camera that isn't broken at the time.

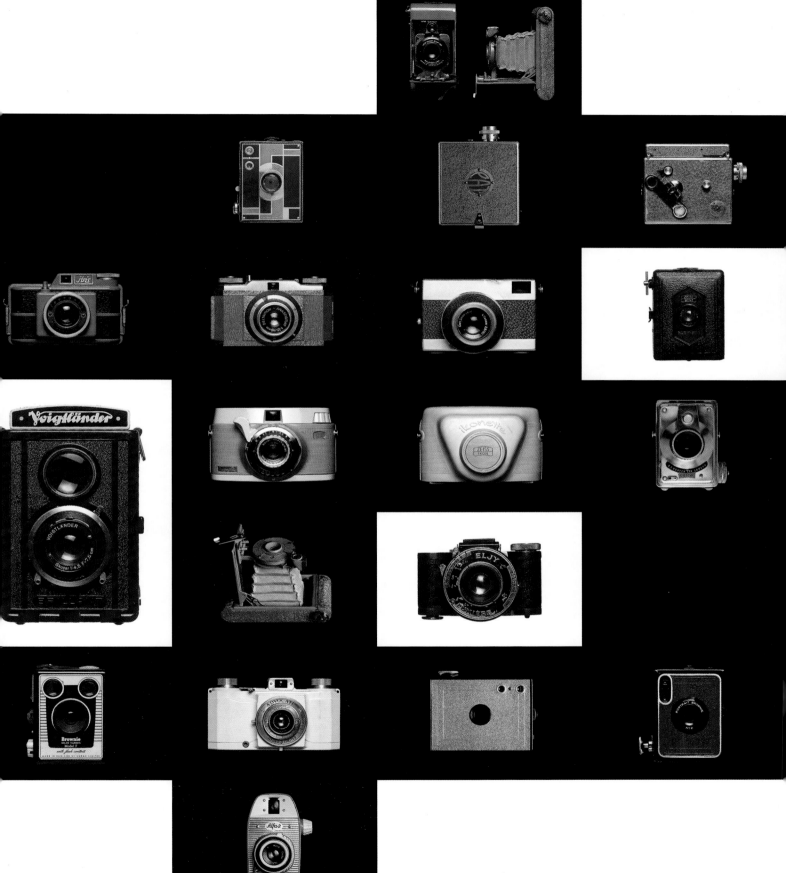

Photography is one of those things that keep me fresh. I hope I've never taken myself too seriously. I base all of my collections on observation, as I'm determined to design clothes not just to please market forces. I believe in the individual, not the corporation.

the room at the top of the shop
interview by hans-ulrich obrist

Obrist: I recently interviewed Hans-Georg Gadamer, the German philosopher. He told me that there was a problem with every recorded interview: the conversation is recorded, but the most important part of it – the silences between the words – are not transcribed. This somehow relates to our conversation earlier, when you said that a fragrance cannot be recorded …

I made a decision to create a Paul Smith fragrance, but of course when you are designing clothes you always have the physical clothes, the touch of the clothes, to talk about and to think about. You are able to put pencil to paper, and describe visually what you are talking about, whether it is a slim-line dress or a long trouser.

Then suddenly you are invited to a fragrance house in Paris, where you sit down with around 20 people, most of them wearing white lab coats. They say, 'Right, Mr Smith, what fragrance do you like?' And then suddenly your arms start to wave around and you're thinking about what fragrance you like, and you know that what you really don't want to do is name an existing brand, so you just go, 'Umm …'

Then they said, 'Well, what food do you like?' And I said, 'I like simple food. I don't like hot and spicy food.' That was a good start. And then they said, 'Where do you like to go a lot? Where do you go on holiday?' And I said, 'I go a lot to Italy and to France. I like to go to Italy because the food is simple but the lifestyle is very nice.' So immediately they started building a picture of what I like, they realised I didn't want a strong fragrance, an attention-seeking one, that you can smell from across the room.

It's a little bit like a phantom image?

That's right. I said I liked the smell of bread, coffee, freshly-cut grass, and then slowly they built up a picture of my tastes, and they realised that I like simple, natural things. I wanted something personal. I remembered that I like aromatherapy oil when I have a bath sometimes. My wife buys it. One kind is for travelling, when you want to relax, and another is for when you want to wake up. This made them think, 'Oh, geranium is a good start, or orange or cedar.'

In *How Nature Works*, Norwegian scientist Per Bak discusses complex systems which have 'feedback loops'. Your development of the Paul Smith fragrances seems like a complex, dynamic system which grew out of your conversations in France.

Yes, and all done just with words. To change the subject for a minute, something that excited me recently was getting a bottle of wine which had a braille label. For blind people, the sense of taste is very important. So the idea of a braille label seemed so obvious, and so interesting.

I was wondering if you could tell me a little bit about your laboratory, the room that we are in today. It's more than just an office …

It's my room. My playroom. In fact, it has become – without me realising – quite a well-known room around the world, because people have heard about it. A Japanese girl requested to come and see me because she wanted to see this office. She had read about it in magazines. While she was here, she chatted to me for ten minutes and took no photographs. Then, two weeks later, she sent an amazingly detailed drawing – done from memory after just ten minutes in my room.

It reminds me of Frances A. Yates's memory machines …
Yes. Just straight in there. Also, we had someone who fixed a
camera in one corner of the room, and photographed it daily,
because she felt it's a bit like a beach, by the sea, where things
drift in and then go away. And because, just as during this
conversation that we are having today, people come and go,
and say, 'Oh, what's this?' and then they move this, and put
that there, and the office sort of moves around. And then
suddenly I see something, and I say 'I've been looking for
that for four days!' and it has just appeared out of nowhere.

The strange thing is that I also have exactly the same amount
of stuff in a container in Nottingham in my warehouse, just as
in this office now, left over from the 'True Brit' exhibition in
Japan. We emptied the office, this room, completely, and put
it into a container, and it was recreated in Kobe and Tokyo.
And I did all my interviews for the exhibition in the office in
Kobe, and sat at the table …

This table?
Yes, and during one interview I discovered a fax from Piers
Gough that I'd been looking for. It was still there, because one
day they had literally come and taken the entire office, like it
is today. They just took it all.

So, it also became like a time machine.
And, apart from this table, it's still all in a container in my
warehouse. When somebody finally opens that up it will be
interesting to see what's actually in there.

How did this eclectic mix of things start?
When was the beginning?
I visit street markets a lot, and antique sales, and I buy things
I like. Toys, books, magazines. Anything. People also know
that I enjoy these sorts of things, so I get sent stuff all the time.
Normally between six and twenty things arrive each day. From
fans around the world. Sometimes details are written on them
saying who has sent them. And sometimes not, but there

might be a little story attached. I try to keep the place tidy and
neat, but because stuff comes so often, it's impossible. Then of
course, the other thing is that everybody loves it, so when they
come here they get very inquisitive. They say, 'Oh, where's that
from?' – you know, like the chicken over there, made from a
black rubbish sack, from Cape Town. There's a story attached
to a lot of the things as well, which is great if you're having
meetings. It makes everything light. When people interview me,
I can see them smiling at something they've noticed. The doll's
house is made from Christmas cards from two years ago, and
we have a garage for the doll's house, next to it, made from
last year's Christmas cards and …

It's also a recycling machine!
Exactly. And these boxes, and all those drawers, are full of
things to do with graphic design. Envelopes, notebooks. On
the sofa there is a collection of leather jackets. There are
plastic animals on the television for some reason. There is no
reason for all this stuff really, apart from the fact that it just
happens naturally. I've never ever tried to do anything with it.
I just arrive, sit there, and it happens.

**That's what Whistler once said, that 'Art happens'. But
what is also interesting are the unexpected encounters,
because whenever I visit your office, your laboratory –
I still don't know what to call it – you call it a room.**
Just a room. Paul's room. The room at the top of the shop.

**So whenever I visit Paul's room, it is the unexpected,
surprising encounters that strike me.**
Do you remember the chocolate cake the last time you were
here? I brought out some plastic chocolate cake, like this, and
walking up the stairs just then was one of my assistants, with
a slice of real chocolate cake that looked exactly the same.
Amazing. And totally unplanned.

**Different forms of apparently the same thing, meeting
simultaneously on the table.**
Things like that are always happening.

This room gives a new meaning to that horrible word 'headquarters'. 'Headquarters' usually has a cold, corporate connotation, but here it is more like Yates's way. It's the way the mind works, or as Picabia said, 'The head is round shaped so that thinking can change its direction.' Well, that's why you described this room as 'inside Paul's brain', wasn't it?

Each time I visit this room, there is this daily object, from one person who has sent you all these readymades through the post. What is the story of this incredible chain of objects?

An anonymous fan in America sends things, pieces of art, really. A bicycle seat, a skateboard, a traffic cone. All with no packaging, with my address and stamps straight on them. We get sent lots of things that people make. Lots of Japanese people send knitted things; we've had knitted teddy bears, a complete Paul Smith outfit. One woman, Kacchi, from Tokyo, has sent me images of little mannequins she has made, wearing Paul Smith clothes. And she's photographed lifesize versions of some of these in my main shop in Tokyo.

There is a recurrence of certain animals, especially rabbits, isn't there? How did the rabbit collection start?

The rabbit story happened on the train going to Nottingham, in 1984, when I was with an American friend. I was looking out of the window, daydreaming, and he said to me, 'What are you looking at?' And I just made up a story, and said, 'I'm looking for a rabbit, because if I see a rabbit, it's good luck for my new collection.' The following week he sent me a rabbit from America – that one was the first one. And he must have told somebody, who told somebody else, who told somebody else, because now we get sent box-loads of rabbits.

A chain reaction.

Yes, like six to fifteen a week. They just keep coming.

And then there is always at least one new book put on display, and this time it's Naomi Klein, *No Logo*. Is that the book that you're reading right now?

Yes, I read parts of it, and then I stopped, because in a way it's so similar to the way I ... I've always got the latest book here, but I don't necessarily read them all. I don't know how I get them, or where they come from, they just appear. Naomi Klein's book was interesting to me because it is very much about what I've been talking about. For instance, I've been looking for a building for a second shop in New York. I'm attracted by the commercial side of SoHo, downtown, but emotionally I don't want to be there. It's because I'm trying to continue to pioneer individuality. I think it used to exist a lot, but it doesn't any more, because people are so accepting of capitalism and of the way other companies just 'roll-out' a single concept in all their shops. That is in many ways what Klein's book is about ...

… and about the exploitation of workers in the Third
World by global brands.

Exactly, that's what I mean. The problem is that money is the
only thing that really talks, and in a business like fashion it is
quite challenging to constantly be the independent one,
because Paul Smith is an independent company.

Were there ever any friendly or unfriendly takeover offers?

There have been a lot over the last three years. There were
several companies interested in Paul Smith Limited. They
can't take me over, because we're an independent company,
not a public company, but they bombard you with offers and
tell you the advantages, and then your staff think, 'We could
open twenty shops in three years, and we can do this, and
we can do that'. But this office, in a way, reflects the way the
company is, and the way I am. Which is just very … get on
with it, you know? I love it. And that's the difference.

And I think that your job, as Edward de Bono says, always
changes you, but you never change the job. That's something
I've been aware of since I was about 22 years old. I have
always been determined to remain independent. Obviously, as
you get older, the difficult thing is health and energy. I probably
will have to decide whether I get somebody else involved,
eventually, but at the moment I really am on a push to pioneer
individuality. So my new Milan shop is different from my London
shop, and if I open more shops in Paris or New York they will
be different from the Milan one. I'm really trying not to be
marketing-led, and not be sucked in to the American way
of money, money, money, power, power, power.

To break this homogenisation tendency?

Yes. People walk into this office, thinking they are going to find
a chic designer office, and I'm sometimes nervous that they are
going to think I'm not serious. But Sally Brampton, an English
writer, once said, 'Be careful when you go to Paul Smith's room,
because sometimes people think he's childish. In fact he's

childlike, and the difference is enormous.' And if that's true –
if I am childlike – then that's fantastic, because if you are
childlike you've always got a fresh approach to everything.
If I can do that, great!

**I think Robert Louis Stevenson once said, 'It is all about
play, but with the seriousness of playing children'.**

Yes, that's great. That's perfect.

**In their book *Empire*, Toni Negri and Michael Hardt write
not only about different spatial zones, but also about
different temporalities. And that's obviously about
resisting the tendency towards homogenisation over time.
We've talked already about your 'time machine', and how
when one enters this room, one also enters a different
notion of time.**

I don't know what it is. I wonder if I want to be independent
because I'm spoilt. Since the age of 21 I've been my own boss,
and I'm maybe surrounded by subservience. Maybe I'm not
good at taking orders. Sometimes I think that's the problem,
and maybe one day that will become my enemy. Or it may be
that I'm not brave enough to become bigger. I hope it's not that,
but I think it could be, a little bit. But I also think I can just do
everything without being too predictable.

I've never been a drug taker or a person looking for escapism
or the obvious route. If I can cope with life, on my terms, with
my head intact in a normal way, then that's pretty interesting.
A lot of people are tempted by the predictable route of
becoming part of a big conglomerate, and getting their shop
in the main street, and that just doesn't interest me.

That's also about the unexpected.

Yes, and also the challenge of fighting from behind. I think I'm
like David Coulthard in the Grand Prix last weekend. His car
didn't start, he was 20 seconds back, and then he ended up
fifth. I think I'm always at the back because I don't have the
power and the money of the big brands. But I always end up

pretty near the top, in terms of respect, in my industry.

I think I've worked hard, without realising it, at not being fashionable – but then I'm not *not* fashionable, either. I'm just tucked under being fashionable. And I am pleased that sometimes when I go to places where I meet artists, I'm the only fashion designer there. I seem to be thought of in a different way from most fashion designers. We're in a fashionable business, where being fashionable is important, and yet we're not fashionable. And we're still relatively important within the world of fashion, not necessarily in money terms, but in terms of the respect people give us.

It was interesting when Rem Koolhaas asked you this morning if you know Miuccia Prada, and you said you hadn't met her. So you're not spending most of your time in the fashion world?

That's true. Often it's more interesting to meet people from outside fashion. I'm most proud of sticking by my own ideas, and not allowing myself to be sucked down the usual path of fashion designers. I think I'm really disappointed by the way the world is going now, with everybody wanting to move so fast, and nobody allowing enough time to gain the experience that you need to do things well. In some ways it's good, because it means in theory that people are taking more risks. In fact, though, they are not, because everything is so safe now. You know, there's that Italian motorbike rider. He's 21 and a breath of fresh air in the Grand Prix, because he is suddenly winning, and he is cheeky and naughty and he's got green hair and lives in Belgravia, a posh neighbourhood here in London. His team rented him a special circuit to try a new bike out, which was very costly, and the day before the trial was his 21st birthday so he had a hangover and he couldn't do it. They were furious with him, but then he went on to win the next three races anyway. In a way, it's terrible, but good for him! And I think about the use of computers and the Internet and e-mail,

and I thank goodness there are still some human beings left, because at least we argue or disagree, or we're happy or we're sad, or we have a reaction.

What is the importance of drawing for your work? Has the computer changed the way you design clothes?

I am a little sad about the disappearance of pencil and paper, especially in the world of architecture. Obviously, I know that the Guggenheim in Bilbao could not have been created without a computer, because of the shapes, but at least Frank Gehry did his pencil-work first, to give an impression of what he wanted. And there is Cy Twombly, 'taking his pencil for a walk', as he used to say. Like everything in life, there should be a balance between the modern way and the more traditional way. With architecture, you've got to understand the formal procedure. With fashion, you've got to understand about pattern-cutting, about production methods, about how garments are made. Then if you want to reject them, that's fine, but you have to have knowledge in order to reject or edit.

I'm still interested in working out this balance, and a lot of the stuff in this room is to do with my work. It gives me ideas and makes me laugh. If you look at my shop windows, there is always humour to be found in them.

You invent these ideas for window displays?

I work with a man named Lance Martins. We work on them together, which is great. And Lance sometimes travels to my shops abroad to work on window displays, especially in Asia, to encourage shop managers to come up with their own ideas, which Lance can develop with them.

One of the things about this office is the amazing urge that people have, not only to look, but also to move the objects around. I want to ask you about participation in relation to the office, and in relation to your work.
How do you see participation in relation to clothing and to fashion?

I can turn the question on it's head, if that's alright. People often say to me, 'Do you consider your work art?' I say that I don't consider it art, but that the clothes definitely do a job. You don't necessarily participate in the clothes, but the clothes help you out, they make you feel cheerful, they make you feel serious. If you were to get onto a 747 jet, and you met the pilot at the door, and he was wearing beach clothes and a hat, even though he completely had the skills to fly you across the Atlantic, would you trust him to do that? So clothes really do a job; the strength of a uniform is amazing, it makes you feel important and strong.

Can you tell me about your unrealised projects?
What are the 'unbuilt roads' of Paul Smith?

Last week I had an interesting conversation with Mr Cappellini, of the Italian furniture company, and it may be interesting to enter a world which I know little about. Maybe with lateral thinking, and a sense of naivety, I might be able to come up with something special. It might take a little time. But I don't have any big plans you know. I enjoy today and tomorrow, and getting on with today and tomorrow.

Of course we need to move forward and to progress, and we need to work hard for our staff, but there is so much you can contribute every day, in conversation, in energy. Nobody leaves this office without an injection of energy, I assure you. And they arrive probably, in some cases, slightly nervous, if they're doing an interview, or whatever. But they always leave with a positive energy, and a strength.

If that's the only thing I can contribute, that's fine with me.

return to sender

Objects sent through the post from
an admirer in Aqueboge, New York

June 1998 – February 2001

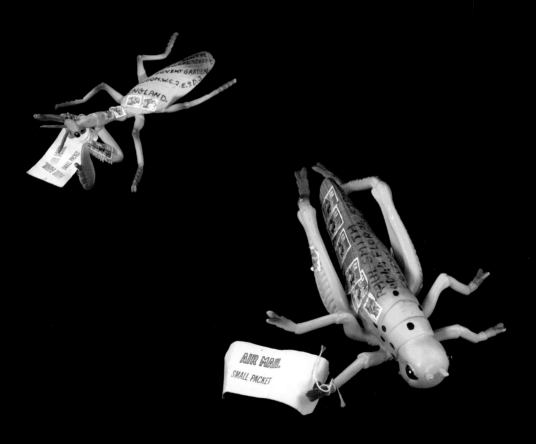

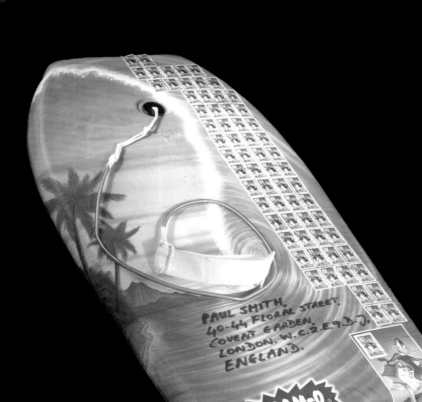

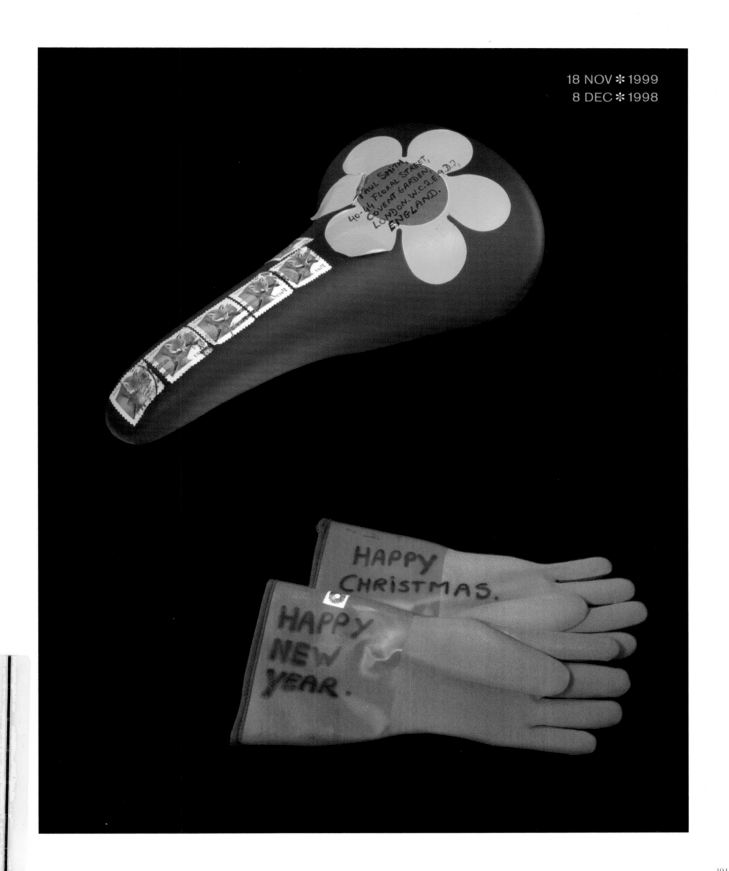

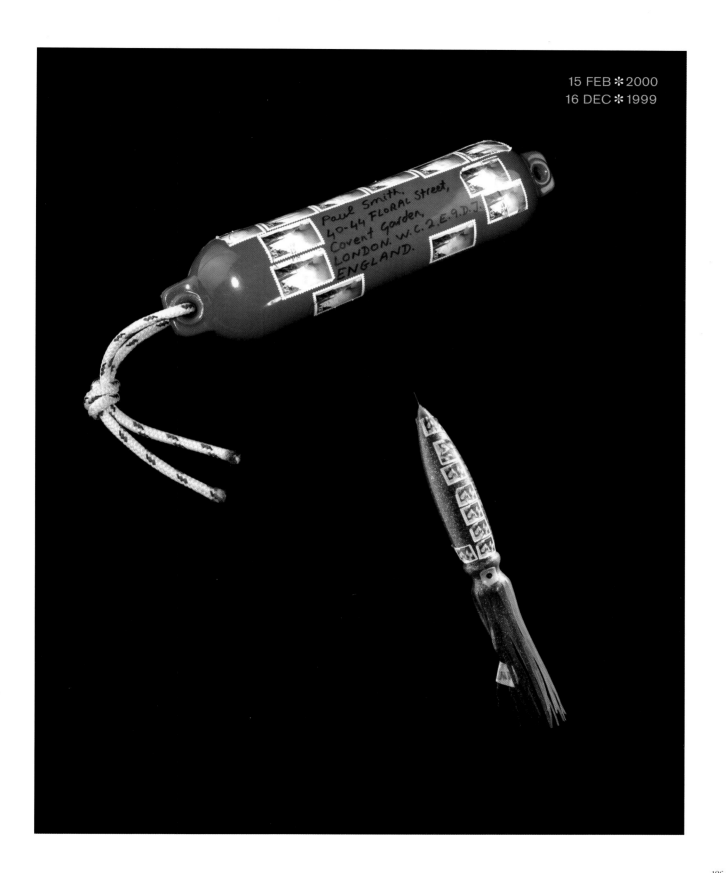

Sir Paul Smith
40–44 Floral Street
London WC2E 9DG
England

Photocopy this address label and post your own object to Paul Smith.
No packaging necessary. Please affix postage.

paul smith lives
james flint

It was awful
when it happened.

Oh yes.
It was terrible.

It was a real shock.

You can't imagine.

He slipped you know.

Slipped and fell.

So it wasn't suicide?

Suicide?

Of course it wasn't suicide.

My God!

How could anyone think that?

But the press.

Fuck the press.

The press are idiots.

If those journalists had bothered
to talk to a single person who was
close to him …

… a single one!

Then they would have
told them straight away.

That Paul didn't kill himself.

What a ridiculous idea.

Offensive, in fact.

Totally so.

…

… …

So. Er. Well. …

So how did it happen?

…

…

It was the toad.

The toad?

The rubber one, that he'd put in
that small hole in the floorboard
just by the stairs. As a joke.

Everyone loved that little toad.

Oh yes. Everyone did. It was
typical of Paul, to take something
small like that …

… something so small …

… just a wee little toad

… and make it into a feature.

A talking point.

Without a thought to his own
personal safety.

Not a thought. But then that was
Paul all over, see.

Always putting other people first.

Always others.

We really miss him.

It's true. We do.

But that toad's at the bottom
of the spiral stairs, right?
So I don't understand.
How could he trip on the toad and
fall *down* the stairs, if the toad was
at the bottom?

It makes no sense. Ah, well, you see. That was just
the thing. The toad wasn't in its
hole when he tripped on it.

Wasn't in its hole?

No. It wasn't.

It had been moved.

Moved.

Moved?

Moved. What happened was … … what happened was
David and Iman came by …

… just dropped in to say hello, like
they often did. Old friends, you know.

Oh yes. Old, old friends. And they
brought Cephallonia with them.

Their great-granddaughter.

Poor old David, on a Zimmer
frame he was, poor old thing.

Had a terrible time,
getting up the stairs.

Not the spiral stairs?

No! Not the spiral stairs. The main
stairs, the ones Paul lined with
photographs, the ones that came
up onto the landing that led to the
office and the spiral stairs.

The landing with
the hole in it?

The hole. And. Therefore.

The toad?

Precisely.

David would never have got up
the spiral stairs.

Not at his age.

It was more than he could
have possibly managed. But he
was determined to get up the
other stairs, the ones that led
to the office.

And the landing?

And the landing.

Very determined, David is.

Was.

Yes. Was.

Well you could see that
from his career, couldn't you? The dear.
All those changes.

But I still don't understand?

About Cephallonia?

Look. It's really very simple.
They'd left her on the landing, you
see, while Paul and Iman went to
help David get up the stairs …

… left her to play …

… and she'd found the toad …

… the toad in its hole …

… the hole where it'd been sitting
for years …

… gathering dust.

And she took it out …

… she took it out …

… said afterwards she only wanted
poor toadie to be free …

… poor toadie to be free …

… took him out and put him on
the stairs …

… the other stairs,
the ones with the photographs, the
ones David was slowly climbing up,
with Iman going before him and
Paul behind.

To steady him, you see.

Exactly. To steady him.

And no one saw the toad?

No one saw the toad.

Iman stepped over it and David
stepped over it but poor Paul …

… poor Paul …

He slipped and fell?

Slipped and fell.

Slipped and fell.

Head over heels.

A tragedy.

Slipped and fell.

The dear.

Well, he always was a touch
accident prone.

More than a touch!
The man was a klutz!

Oh that's unfair.

But I didn't mean it nastily.
You're forgetting the talent he had
for turning almost any disaster into

Well I suppose that's true. a triumph.
I mean the whole thing started with
an accident.

The whole thing?

Being a designer,
Oh, you mean the the business, everything.
cycle crash?

When he was sixteen? Yes. Of course. What else?

Yes yes, that's right. Surely you've
Yes, it was the first thing … done your research?

… he was very big into bicycle
Oh yes. Very big. racing, Paul.
And very fit.

He was a teenager Extremely fit.
then, of course.

And all the fitter for it. Naturally.

Have you seen the photographs? Absolutely.
Well, I've seen some of them …

We could get them out!
Not now, Gerry. I don't think Let's get them out.
that's what the young man's here
to talk about.

Maybe later? Er … we could look But it wouldn't take a …
at them a little later on. I'd rather
get on and talk about the Beach.

Of course you would.
So. Can we talk about the Beach? Of course.

Yes. Well, we were just
coming to that.

Okay.
So. Is the tape rolling?
Or the memory chip or whatever?
I know, I know, I'm so hopelessly
retro. It's just how I am … It is?
So we're ready? Okay. So. Hello.
My name is Derbias Frenelle …

He means Derbert Frenell.

Thanks, Gerry. No. Really.
Thanks. At least I'm not named
after a has-been millennial pop
diva that can't even sing.

She can too.

She so cannot.

Well it's the nodules, isn't it?
She's got nodules.
Like Elton John.

Nodules my aunt. She could never
sing, not from the first. Well at least my mother
chose the name for me.

Oh you bitch. How dare you bring
my mother into this!

I didn't say anything about your
mother. You brought her up.

I did not.

You so did. All I said was …

Whoa, hey. Hold up. Time out.
Look, I'm sorry to interrupt,
but does it really matter?
I mean, right now? As far as I'm
concerned, you can call yourselves
whatever you like.
It doesn't make any difference to
the interview. Derbert, Derbias,
whatever. I really don't give a shit.

Ooo, listen to him,
getting all testy.

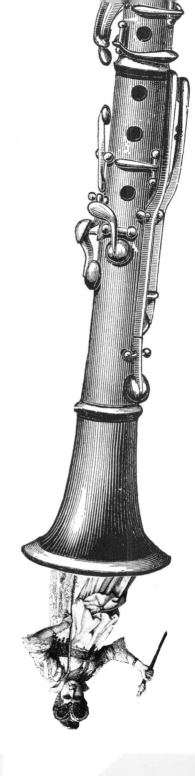

Umm. So easily roused. Would you
like a cold drink? There's some
nice iced tea in the fridge.

No, no it's alright. I'm sorry.
Really. I over-reacted. But can we
get on? We're running a
little short on time.

Oh, okay. So. My name is …
Derbias Frenelle, and I'm 28 years
of age, no comment needed from
you, thank you, Gerry. And I've
been with PS for just under five
years now. I am one half English,
one third Sri Lankan and one sixth
Burmese. I was conceived in
Cannes, born in Lagos and
educated at the American school in
Tangiers, before moving over here
to rainy old England. Over my
teenage years I shall, if you don't
very much mind, draw a veil;
suffice it to say that in 2013, at the
precocious age of 22, I graduated
from Sussex with a Masters
in Predictive Couture, which
makes me almost as intelligent
as I am handsome.
Before working for Paul I did
some time with another designer,
over which I'll also draw a veil if
you don't very much mind.
A sluttish-looking one in crocheted
steel wire, with integrated razor
blades. Ha ha ha. Sorry.
Just my little joke.

Only if you wipe Gerry's comment
so that we can start over.

Okay. Okay. […] Fine. It's been
wiped. Okay? Let's try it again.

Sure you wouldn't like
some tea?

No. Yes. I'm sure. No. Thank you.
Derbias?

Yes?

Please?

Okay. Thank you, Derbias.
Gerry?

My name's Gerry Halliwell.
I'm 25, and I'm from
Huddersfield.
…
… … Don't sulk Gerry.
It doesn't become you.

Gerry, why don't you tell me about the Beach?

Are you sure?

Yes, I'm sure. It's what I've come all this way to talk about.

No. I mean are you sure you wouldn't rather Derbias did it?

Well, you know Gerry, between you and me it's quite hard to get Derbias to talk about anything other than himself. Not that he's not an interesting character, of course. But his character isn't the primary focus of this interview. So I thought that maybe if we could get started while he's out of the room … ? Then maybe he'll be encouraged to join in when he gets back.

Well, if you're sure.

Go ahead. Please.

Okay. Erm, well … Well it's all so complicated! I don't really know where to begin.

How about at the beginning? Tell me what you know about how the whole thing got started.

Well I can only tell you what I've been told.

Is it stuff that Paul told you?

I guess it is.

Then that's fine.

Okay.

Well. As far as I'm aware, the Beach, what we all call the Beach, what Paul called the Beach, got started by accident. Another Paul accident. That's what made Paul so good, really. His ability to improvise.

Go on.

The way he told it to me was that he was always a hoarder. Same as his Dad, apparently – growing up, he told me once, there was always all this stuff lying around, cluttering up the house.

Stuff?

You know. Stuff. Useful junk. Odds and ends. Piles of photos, piles of decorating stuff, offcuts of wood, bags of seashells, boxes of magazines, bags of clothes.

Why didn't Paul's Dad just throw all this stuff away?

Because he liked making things. Weird things. Like once he made a shoehorn. I mean, who makes a shoehorn? No one, right? But Paul's Dad did. Needed one one day and so made one out of a couple of bits of wood and some old wire. Used to keep it hanging on a wall-peg in the hallway. Visitors would ask, like, what's that weird thing? 'Oh, that's just Dad's shoehorn', Paul would have to say. It all sounds a bit strange, if you ask me.

Kooky.

Well. You know. If you prefer. But they were from Nottingham, not Tennessee.

His old man was a bit of a photographer, wasn't he?

Oh yeah. Very much so. Amateur, but very good. Had a real eye. And a painter too – one of the things we've got up in the permanent collection is a painting he made on a pebble.

Cool. Is it nice?

Yeah, it is, kind of.

And so you think this is where Paul got it from? I mean the thing about hoarding things.

I guess so. I mean, where else?

Because when he had his first shop up in Nottingham …

… things he'd been collecting. Things like penknives, erasers, exercise books. That kind of thing. Stuff he bought on holiday. Anything. **And so what happened next?**

Well what happened was, pretty soon some of Paul's friends started picking up on this habit of his and started sending him more stuff. Just odd little things they thought he'd like. Not expensive things, generally, although sometimes they were. Cheap things. Normal things, but things which had something about them. Things which were unusual, or were kitsch or cute, or that had some nice colour combination or design. One woman got into sending things completely unwrapped. A road cone, with the address written on it in marker pen, and the stamps stuck on. A surfboard. A bundle of twigs, with Paul's address and 'Merry Christmas' written on them. A stuffed mountain goat. **And this carried on when he moved down to London and opened the shop in Floral Street?**

Well, I think that's where it got going properly, really. When he got to London. He started putting some of the items in display cabinets in the shop, marking them for sale. **What sort of items?**

He'd go through stages. Clock radios maybe, often ones that didn't work. Snowstorm shaker toys. Wind-up watches. Old fountain pens. Toy robots – robots were a favourite. Rabbits, of course. Rabbits became something of an obsession. **Rabbits?**

Oh yeah. He was on some train trip with a buyer, once, looking out of the window, and the guy said, you know, 'What're you looking for?' And without really thinking about it Paul said, 'Oh, a rabbit, because if I see a rabbit then I know the new collection will sell really well'. Which was nonsense. he'd just made that up in order to have something to say. But the next thing he knew the guy had sent him a stuffed rabbit, and told everyone he knew that Paul Smith had this big rabbit superstition, and from then on it was rabbits rabbits rabbits, everywhere. We still get about three or four a day at least. **That's insane.**

Oh yes. Completely. But it was because of things like that Paul began to realise the power he had. And soon after he started to trigger his first trends. **Trends?**

Trends. Like the Filofax. It was
Paul who rediscovered Filofaxes,
which had been around for, like,
a century, and started to sell them
in the store. Before anyone knew
it they'd become like the personal
accessory of the 1980s. Or boxer
shorts. He was the first person to
start selling boxer shorts in the UK.
Or Dyson vacuum cleaners – the
inventor James Dyson was an old
friend of his, and Paul used to sell
Dual-Cyclones out of Floral Street.
Again, long before they became
so popular.

**Did he sell all the stuff
that people sent him?**

Oh no. I mean, most of it he
just let pile up in his office. He and
the people in his team – because
Paul, you know, wasn't a trained
designer, I mean his wife, Pauline,
taught him most of what he knew
about formal principles and he
didn't draw or anything, what
he did was more conceptual.
He worked in partnership with
people like Derek Morton.

Derek Morton?

You've not heard of Morton? Oh,
Morton was quite brilliant.
He worked for Paul for years.
Brilliant designs. Totally bizarre.

Anyway, where were we?

Er … the beginnings of the Beach
… stuff piling up in Paul's office …
the team …

Oh, that's right. So, with all this
stuff washing up like flotsam –
which is why it first got called
the Beach by Sonia Peric,
a photographer Paul knew – then
Paul's team started to use the
objects like a kind of ideas pool.
A lot of what Paul did, especially,
was like collage. Like, you know,
a black-and-red triangular design
on a polo helmet might inspire
a colour combo for a V-necked
sweater. Or the lining of a suitcase
might trigger an idea for the lining
of a jacket. That kind of thing.
Anything. The window-dresser
might select two or three objects
that looked good together and use
them as the basis for a window
display. Other members of the
team might raid the Beach for ideas
for a catalogue design, or even an
entire clothing range. It's hard to
describe quite how this worked, but
once you saw it in action, the
process was ob …

Hello you two. Are we having fun?

Oh, hi, Derbias. Is that tea?

What else, what else. Clear a space,
Gerry, clear a space. Now.
Shall I be mother?

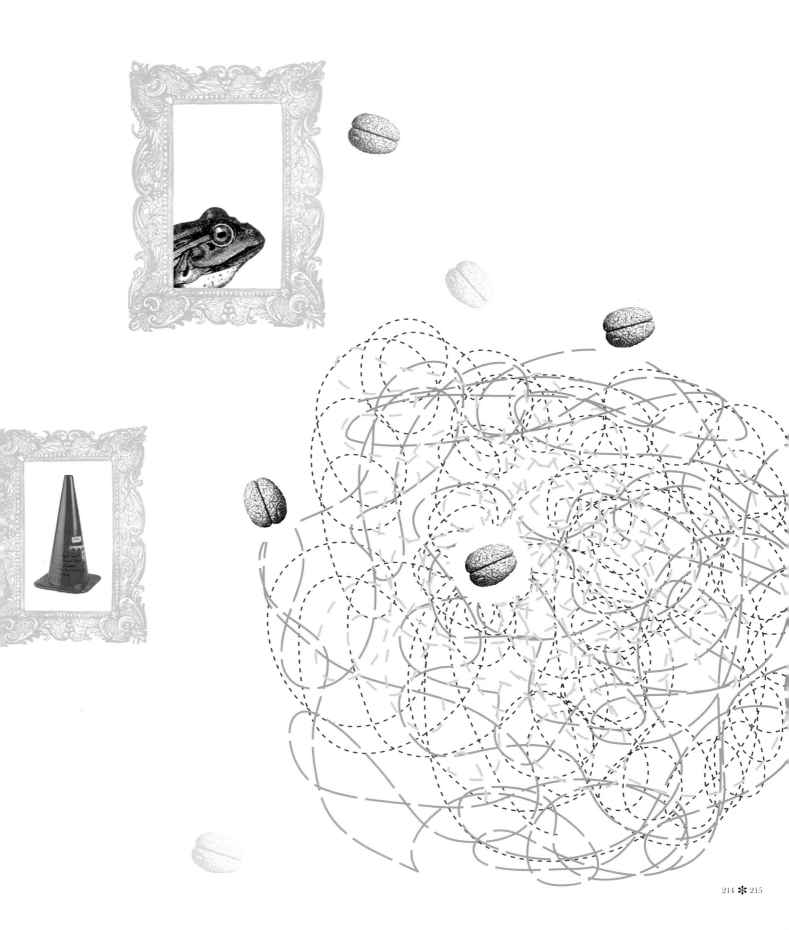

Gerry and me were
talking about the Beach, Derbias.
Gerry's just been telling me how it
all got started. We'd sort of got to
the point where so much stuff had
begun coming in that Paul had
started to shift it back to
Nottingham once a year, where it
went into a permanent collection.

Tell him Gerry.

I really don't want to.

Well if you don't I will.

Go on then.

Yes?

Oh I hate the word
permanent collection.

A 'cornellator'.

You do?

A 'cornellator'?

I do. How many times
do I have to remind you, Gerry,
that permanent collection
is completely the wrong
term to use?

Exactly.

What do you prefer to call it?

After the artist Joseph Cornell?

Well that's the
crucial question, isn't it?

Precisely.

The New York Times called it
a 'collator'.

And why don't you
like that, Gerry?

Well they would. But it gives
completely the wrong idea of how it
works. As well as being terribly
outdated – and not in a good way,
like myself. But Gerry came up
with a nice re-version of it, even
though he refuses to acknowledge
how good it is himself.
Didn't you Gerry?

I just think it's … it's too restrictive
that's all. I mean, Cornell collected
all this stuff like Paul did, for sure,
but he hoarded it and put it into
boxes, whereas as much as he could
Paul put all the things that came
his way back into circulation.

But you see, I just don't agree with
this – I think Cornell did put
things back into circulation. Just in
a different way.

I may have come up with it,
but I don't like it.

I know you don't like it,
but I don't understand why not.

It's marvellous. I think it's dumb.

What is it?

So what term would you prefer,
Gerry, if you had the choice?

Gerry prefers this atrocious joke
word that I thought up one day.

And what's that? A 'mutilator'.

And why do you prefer that?

Because it reminds him of
William Gibson's Wintermute.

But wasn't Wintermute an AI that made Cornell boxes?

Derbias, please – let Gerry answer […] Yeah, in the story. for himself. That's right.

So what's the difference between a man doing it, and a machine? I dunno. I haven't really worked that out. It just seems that, you know, while Cornell was making these boxes because he was a bit of a weirdo, and, you know, lived with his mother, and had a problem with women and all of that, Wintermute made them because, being an intelligence that didn't, like, have any parental hang-ups, it just seemed like the most obvious way for it to correspond with the world around it.

That makes no sense to me at all. I just don't see the difference. And anyway, Cornell wasn't a weirdo, as you so indelicately put it … He suffered from Asperger's syndrome; he was deeply autistic. I don't think there was ever an official diagnosis …

Oh, he was. It's so obvious! Well, whatever, but go on Gerry. There's not much to say. I just like the idea that the machine might have sort of less programming than the human being.

But to me the process is the process, it's the same either way. Wintermute corresponds with the world, Cornell corresponds with the world, the process, the product is the same. I don't see how one system might be purer or more authentic than the other. Maybe you're right. I don't know.

Maybe the terms are both part right and part wrong? Maybe they are.

Maybe so. More tea, anyone?

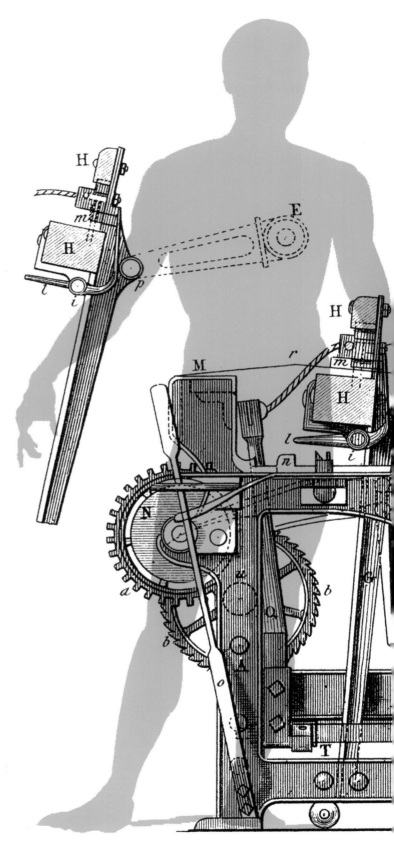

A Pauline van Mourik Broekman
collage.

A small paper and cotton model … A model of Sputnik I, made
of a helium nucleus. from a hamster exercise ball.

A BMW Isetta model car. A model motorbike made out of
pieces of Heineken beer cans.

An octagonal 'oil globe' depicting A white furry toy dog wearing
sea with windsurfers. sunglasses with red frames.
A box containing
cufflinks by Kigu of London.
A 'Big Mouth Billy Bass' rubber
fish on wall mount.
…
…
…
… A treatise on the necessity and
efficacy of a space elevator.
…
…

A round shaped yellow handbag
with raffia detail in the design of
a cat's face, containing samples
of silk fabric.
A Gymnic yellow ball.
A framed note re: Lou and Tara's
visit to David Bailey's Studio,
23rd June 1999.
A folder from Milan, September
2010 Film Festival.

Seven four-inch-square pictures
all depicting different fish.
An inflatable globe. A tape machine
designed to look like a robot.

A framed black-and-white
photograph of a woman and two
girls in traditional dress 'in Golden
Triangle, North Thailand.'
A metal clothes horse, twisted into
breast shapes.
…
…
Four bronze ornate pieces depicting
baskets, one with smaller barrels
fixed around it with ropes.

A 'Slack Key:
The Best of Hawaiian' CD. A Japanese firework.

Four rolls of posters from
Aix en Provence,
for teaching school children. A glass case containing the body
of Damien Hirst, suspended in
A translucent pink bedside–lamp in formaldehyde solution.
the shape of a rabbit.
A framed Bianchi cycling shirt,
in white and sky-blue.

A Jocelyn Warner
wallpaper sample book.

A small, plastic figurine of the
actor Nicholas Cage, with pins A tin toy drumming rabbit.
stuck in it.
A handpainted biscuit tin
A framed painting depicting a depicting George VI and
cartoon of Aaron C. Aardvark at Queen Elizabeth in 1937.
a house party.
… A rubber chicken.
…
A 'Mandruzzato' paperweight.
A box of John Lennon CDs. A snow globe depicting Antwerp.

A Fabergé egg.
An empty wine bottle 'U. F. Off: The Best of the Orb'
with photograph of CD.
Mussolini on the label.
… A matching pair of walruses
by G.H. Laurent.
An International Forum of
Publishers Lifetime Achievement
Award inscribed with the name
Combined manual / guarantee / of Robert A. Violette.
insurance policy for a jaw-implant
mobile telephone.

An imitation Batonka sacred A signed photograph of
stave from Zimbabwe. Dennis Tito.

A souvenir concrete chip from the collapsed Grand Coulée Dam.

A carved wooden model of a conker. Issue 87 of *mute* magazine.

A penis gourd, from Irian Jaya (boxed).

An American orange road cone.

A 'Bowie: Seven Decades' music chip. ... A loose-leaf book of drawings by Sophie Dutertre, with comic

An Apple G9 (boxed); captions in French. accompanied by a card reading: ...

'Paul, here's another one – ... best wishes, Jony Ive.' ...

...

A Benveniste home medical

A film-of-the-book paperback dispensary. edition of 'The Impressionist', ... by Hari Kunzru. ...

... ...

... A lamp with metal base and polar ... bear removable glass lid.

A black album of vintage graphics ... for the branding of cigarettes and ... other products. ...

... A vintage antique coat stand with ... the top missing.

An access all areas security pass for ... Auckland fashion week, 2015. ...

A wooden box containing piece of pottery by Mashiko Yaki.

A framed portrait of Paul by Sergei Sviatchenko. A Vitra Design Museum CD-Rom entitled: '100 Masterpieces'.

A black-and-white photograph of Sean Penn peeing. A small wax-sealed vial containing two hairs from the head of Alexander McQueen.

A plastic-shark-headed pick-up stick.

A Michael Owen 'Soccer Skills' videocassette.

A framed black-and-white ... A signed print of photograph of a topless blonde Robin Bagilhole's 'Flock' woman by Scavullo.

A box of lavender soaps by Carla Mazzei. ... A PlayStation V Holocentre.

Two pairs of skis.

A vintage toy in the form of nine somersaulting monkeys. A hand-written vellum diary entitled: *The Secret Life of*

A water pistol *H. Rosenius.* in the shape of an elephant.

A Ballito ankle-clinging hosiery holder.

A Crosby, Stills, Nash and Young 'American Dream' audio cassette. A crash test dummy and car ...

... A box of skittles. A signed photograph of Elaine Pyke playing the female lead in Steven Spielberg's surprise smash Broadway musical version of 'Macbeth'.

A skeleton hand.

A Fugi magic rope trick.

A paper bag filled with assorted rubber insects.

A Giggle Wiggle game.

A knighthood.

A black-and-white framed photograph of Mick Jagger, wearing only a small pair of shorts

A sponge Postman Pat. and carrying a bucket and spade.

Two Japanese mini kites.

A framed photograph taken at Glastonbury in 1997 showing a black T-shirt with the words 'Paul A pack of 'Welcome to Wyoming' Spliff' printed on it. playing cards.

... A Concorde in-flight

A first edition of James Flint's toiletry pack.

Booker-prize winning novel *The New Pirotechnia*; signed by the A copy of *GQ* magazine, author: 'To Paul, with love'. September 2008.

The Observer's Book A 10th anniversary of the *of Automobiles* (edited by death of Princess Diana Dick Williams). commemorative halo.

A Buckaroo game. ... A travel iron

A $100 Las Vegas poker chip. A partridge in a pear tree.

... ?

... That last one was a joke.

With ever more stuff coming in, with more and more people – no longer just friends and acquaintances but customers and admirers and people who'd just heard about the idea – getting involved, the Beach started to outgrow not just Paul's office in Floral Street but the warehouse in Nottingham as well. A new space was needed. A special space. Somewhere more suitable to the spirit of the enterprise than some steel-frame barn off the M1. And that was when Paul came up with the idea of the caves.

The caves?

The caves. Nottingham's built on sandstone, you see, and the ground underneath the city centre is riddled with them. … ?

It's a nice story. In olden days, if a man ended up penniless, without an income or a home, one of his options was to take his family to Nottingham, borrow a pick and a shovel, and dig himself a cave to live in. Lots of people did this – by the sixteenth century there was a whole community there, living like that.

A sort of human warren.

Exactly. The Victorians cleaned it up of course, because by that time it had become a breeding ground for disease and crime … … which the Victorians didn't like …

Shopping centre built on the site of Nottingham's famous caves, photographed from the air in *Millennium Map* (getmapping plc).

… not at all … … and the caves got forgotten about …

… fell into complete disrepair …

… filled up with water and/or rubbish …

… or just got built on …

That's right. In the 1960s they built a big shopping centre over the few caves that remained. And apart from one or two that were kept open for tourists to gawp at, everyone forgot about them. Then, in 2012, when the shopping centre was demolished, Paul bought the land.

He was fabulously rich by then. He'd never sold the company, see. Fabulously!

And he decided to return to Nottingham and dig out the caves, see what he might find.

It was all still in his hands.

He found a lot.

As it turned out the caves were much more extensive than anyone had ever suspected.

– Much more.

New shafts and passages were discovered, huge underground caverns, an underground lake …

… it was a miracle the town centre hadn't collapsed in on itself, with all this empty space beneath it.

A miracle. So Paul excavated all the caves, and since he'd outgrown his warehouse decided to use them as the new home for the Beach.

He opened them up. cleaned them out, fitted them with watercourses and electricity and goods-lifts and loading bays … … there was enough room down there to store as much stuff as he could possibly imagine. Which is the point at which he brought us in to manage it.

Well, he brought Derbias in.

And a year or two after that I brought in Gerry.

And so that's what you do, is it, the two of you? You curate the caves?

Or manage the Beach.

Or however you want to describe it.

We don't have a real job description, either of us.

We feel it would be counter-productive.

We feel it's important that we remain fluid.

Like the Beach.

Just like.

So is the Beach as important as ever then?

Oh yes! Of course!

More so, I'd say.

Absolutely.

People come and study the Beach, you know. We've got two PhD students writing theses on it now. One philosophy, one economics.

He doesn't mean like fuel, do you Derbias?

Because the Beach is the oil that keeps Paul Smith running.

Hello Dolly!

That's right, I don't mean like fuel. I mean like lubricant.

Gerry, calm yourself.

Well. Look. See. Paul Smith has over 312 hundred outlets in 68 countries worldwide. When a company grows that large, its biggest danger is no longer competition.

How do you mean?

Not at all.

It's itself.

That's right.

It hardens you see.

Meaning that ossification starts setting in.

People get locked into their managerial positions. Their jobs cease to be about innovation … … and become about powerplay.

They concentrate on building empires within the organisation, instead of getting the job done.

Which gets in the way of doing anything actually creative.

The company can't move
fast enough to respond to
new situations. It can try and dictate
them, of course.
Of course – look at the brands.
That's what the brands tried to do.
And it worked, for a while.
By out-sourcing production and
feeding their vast profits back
into marketing they dominated
retail for years … … cutting down on market
flexibility and heterogeneity …
… in the name of
consumer choice. It was all a lie, for the most part.
And the workers got fisted,
naturally.
Though some of them probably
quite liked it.

Just ignore him.
Ultimately it was a first/third world
exploitation thing.
And Paul wasn't prepared
to accept that.
He was positive there
must be another way.

And was there?
Well, you know. Look around.
Paul Smith isn't a brand.

No? It sure looks like one.
I know it looks like one.
But it's not. It's a process.
Kind of a commercial collage.
A way of being-in-the-world.
But without any of that
authenticity bullshit.

And the Beach is central to that?
Absolutely.
It's what keeps it flowing.
And what holds it all together.
Thousands of people send stuff
into us every week, you see …

… and that stuff inspires us.
Meaning it's available for use in
whatever way they want by anyone
who works for the company.
It gets sold on, gets stored, gets
incorporated into designs, gets used
in window displays, or just gets
given away.
Lots and lots of it is given away.
We have a whole charity division
devoted just to that.
Run by a Danish woman
called Helga.
You must meet her.
Yes, yes. I must. So the Beach has
become kind of a redistribution
mechanism?
Well you could describe it as that.
You could describe it as lots of
things. All of them true. I'm sorry, but I'm still
not sure I get it.
Well, I don't mean to be rude,
but you're a journalist, right?
So you're probably pretty well
locked into that intellectual
ownership paradigm.
Even though the best
newspapers and magazines …
… often work in a similar way.
They do?
We think so.
But this is irrelevant right now.
It is? I thought we were just
getting to the heart of the thing.
Well, we are and we aren't.
All you need to understand is,
that by the time of Paul's death,
the Beach had in a sense become
much bigger than him.
Oh most certainly.
It had?

Meaning what, exactly?

Meaning that in a strange sort of
a way the Beach, as the heart of
the company, had – as process –
started to imitate the way Paul's
own mind worked.

Sort of an institutionalised
creative collage.

…
…
…
…
…
…

… I like your suit, by the way.

Oh. Thanks.

A human machine that
incorporated the principles of
creative repetition … … and the joy of the everyday

Boeteng, isn't it?

That's right.

… into its operational fabric.

Which is why we agreed
to talk to you.

…
…
…
…
…

It is?

Because we're actually
getting ready to announce … … on behalf of all Paul Smith
employees …

…
…
…
…
…
…

… that we're to change
the name of the company. You are?

We are.

From simple: 'Paul Smith.'

…
…

Yes. Thought so.

To what?

… To 'Paul Smith Lives.'

'Paul Smith Lives'?

Paul Smith Lives … …
Whaddya think? …
…
…
…
… Well, it's got a certain ring to it,
… I suppose.

poster
my personal possessions
paul smith

observations
and other stuff*

paul smith

*you may want to dig out
your magnifier again.

This text is based on a slide lecture that I normally give to young designers and students, to help them learn to move away from the disease of copying, and away from the notion that everybody in fashion is motivated by money. Design is not just about more and more and more and more! Even though some people call themselves designers, so many of them just imitate.

So this talk starts off in my office, which is full of strange and amusing objects, toys, garments, magazines and books collected around the world and sent to me by friends and strangers alike. Someone once said that I'm 'more childlike than childish', which is absolutely right. I have a very free mind and I never go down the traditional route for anything. You can find inspiration in anything, or everything, and if you can't, you're just not looking properly.

Ideas for design can come from anywhere – I carry a camera with me every day. Here is a photo from a trip I made to Rajasthan, for example. The way Rajasthani women put their clothes together is so fantastic. It can easily inspire how I put my clothes together in a show, or how I might combine those colours in a shirt. But you don't have to go to exotic places like Rajasthan to find ideas.

Here, in Notting Hill Gate, in London, this woman in an extravagant ensemble is on her way to a wedding. Colour is very, very important to me – many of my clothes are simply designed, so colour is a distinguishing characteristic. Many people think colour has to come from some sort of colour board, or particular colour organisation or authoritative hierarchy, but it can come from anywhere. For instance, in this image of an interior from a magazine you could turn the colour scheme into fabric and yarn, and then into knitwear, shirts or whatever. In this range of fabrics, one of the most successful range of fabrics I ever produced,  I drew the colours from traditional dress in Guatemala. I didn't actually copy the fabric; I simply wove these multi-colours, multi-patterns together.

This is an early 1980s collection of Paul Smith shirts, influenced, on the left, by Art Deco, and, on the right, by graffiti. A visit to the Alhambra Palace, Granada, full of mosaics and tiles, inspired this shirt print. In this photograph, from somewhere in Asia, if you put your hand over the bottom part of the woman and look at her face, she's a beautiful girl. But as soon as you put her into an army uniform and cover up her face, then something turns. The power of clothes can make you look important, sexy, severe, tall, thin, fat, whatever. Simply adding zings of colour can be an inspiration for a

stripe around the waist, or a tie, a braiding for a backpack. No reason at all for this

photograph – Teddy boys who saw me in a street in Tokyo.

This woman has to wear a hard hat, but she wears it over a traditional Chinese sun hat.

The pair doesn't actually function properly; every time she moves it wobbles

and it could easily come off. These hats are a perfect example of two things together that

shouldn't be together, which is a constant source of inspiration for me. That approach can

result in the pairing of a pinstripe suit with a wrecked, old, denim shirt; or, in the case of this

book, it could be a very, very posh cover with very low-grade paper inside, or vice versa.

Returning to the use of colour, one of the great masters was Matisse. He often put

colours together that normally aren't seen together, which can create striking moods – cool,

minimalist, eccentric. If you look at this green with this blue, and then at the

same green in the following three images, combined with other colours, it looks, in turn, Pop,

then sophisticated, then the opposite.

Now I come to a key point for the young designer – graphic or product or fashion or

whatever: when they've got this tag 'designer', it's quite a burden for them. So I say, well,

maybe you don't have to think about it quite so deeply; maybe you should be a lot more light-hearted about it. The way you use colour could be a key point. This slide shows a typical colour combination, black and white, a crisp, minimal way of dressing. As soon as you put two hot colours together, suddenly you've got visions of Warhol, Pop Art, clubs, a slightly more eccentric combination; here, you're in the south of France, on a hot day, by the beach, very washed out, indigo.

The wrong thing in the wrong place: we all know this zebra should be black-and-white striped, but he's not. Simply changing the colour or texture of something quite normal turns it into something completely new. For instance, this red coat is what we call a duffel coat in England. In Italy it's known as a Montgomery, after General Montgomery, who wore it during the Second World War, and it should be made in camel or navy blue. But by making it in red, in a cashmere-mix fabric, it suddenly turns into something completely different. When these coats come into the showroom they will be represented in red, navy blue and camel. Making the coat in red, for a show, draws attention to these coats through publicity images, though for commercial reasons, we'll sell most of them in the usual colours. It's the 'classic with a twist' approach, like this Harris Tweed jacket on the left, which should be in a ginger colour, but it's yellow. The wrong things in the wrong place can make a powerful image.

Here is a corduroy suit, which, again, we would sell in quantity in olive or navy blue. But in pink, it grabbed a lot of attention for this collection, and was printed in many newspapers because of its colour. Many young designers get muddled in starting their business because perhaps they only make things like this, and then have nothing to sell. It's a matter of trying to get the balance right between clothes that are for the catwalk and clothes that sell.

This is a traditional English coat called an Epsom, worn to horseraces, always made in olive drab. Putting it into red got it onto the front cover of *Arena* magazine, worn by Bryan Ferry. Obviously, when you come into the showroom, you can have it in olive drab as well. I try to teach students that if they only make classic garments, they probably won't have a business; if they only make avant-garde clothes, they also probably won't have a business. If they get the balance right between these two aims, they'll have a good chance at success.

This photograph was taken in China. One of the security guards at one of the palaces in Beijing, wearing an Yves Klein blue that then went on to be an inspiration for a whole collection in the summer of 1993. And this is simply a traditional Scottish fabric, which has existed for years. But by putting a big pink check over it suddenly it becomes fashionable and different, and it was one of the best selling fabrics that we ever did. This is 1982. Now it is commonplace to see cotton drill or cotton

knitwear in colours. But at the time, just the fact that you were using such bright colours

was unusual. So it's always been very much about colour, like these tanks, for instance,

 which then went on to inspire a pair of day-glo shorts. I'm not sure how you

explain that, but it just came into my head!

These slides are about observation again.  Photographing fish in China and

then turning it into a T-shirt and shorts. And this is a hand-patched eiderdown, which

sparked off an idea based on the fact that people used to repair things rather than replace

them. Now we more often throw things away or give them to charity shops.

So for summer 2000 we designed a whole collection of things that are repaired and mended,

with hand stitching, and so on.

I have turned many other things literally into clothes or accessories: a palette-shaped

button with the texture of dried paint;  postage stamps for a

T-shirt design; fake eyeballs made into cufflinks and buttons – so you've got an eye as a

cufflink and an eye as a button so it's like the idea that you're always watching somebody as

you travel around. And these are spectacles with eyes painted on them.

I remember wearing these standing on the Great Wall of China, asking my incredulous guide to photograph me wearing them. I once had some nice plain socks that weren't selling well, so I took some unused stock postcards, stapled them around the top of each pair, and suddenly the socks sold out. That was a successful experiment in creative packaging. This man is wearing five layers of clothing, in blue, white, lime green, blue and grey. The Chinese put on more and more clothing as it gets colder, rather than just buying one big jacket. That kind of sight can be inspirational when you're putting a fashion show together. Something odd I noticed in Beijing was that some Chinese people leave the labels on the sleeves of their new designer suits. I also saw someone wearing Pierre Cardin spectacles with a tag hanging around his nose. Capitalism meets Communism – they want to show off the Western clothes they have.

This image is simply to illustrate the combination of burgundy and blue, which was important in the Yves Klein show. Traditionally you would never use brown lining in a blue jacket, but I love that mix, and the fact that the jacket is heavily repaired. It was in the Spring 2001 collection.

One of my personal interests is in photo-realism, and in photographic printing generally. This image is obviously the Duomo in Florence.  On closer inspection you realise that it's not the Duomo at all, but an image of it painted onto the side of a bus.  The wrong thing on the wrong thing, which was the direct inspiration for this mini skirt. And it was through this skirt that I got the opportunity to design my own Mini motorcar. An amazing sequence of events.

This was one of the best-selling shirts we ever printed – a rucksack printed life-size onto the fabric, then engineered and cut to end up on the back of the shirt, suggested by a £3 rucksack I bought in Nottingham which lay around my office. You could print apples seen in a street market, or logs, or bananas. You're walking down the street and you could see a box of oranges, like here in Endell Street around the corner from my office in Covent Garden. That could be a shirt, for instance. And this is just an idea – I didn't use this – but it's just an idea to show students that a photograph from the back of a fish tank,  could be a shirt!

I would never copy anything, ever, but in 1982, I got interested again in Kandinsky, whose paintings influence my shirts. Down the road here in Covent Garden there used to be a garden shop, where I'd see seed packets in the window. I don't know why one suddenly thinks 'shirt' when one sees a seed packet – and this is hard to explain to students – but that ended up on a shirt, not literally, but there it is. One of the most important shirts we ever made. And this shirt was, in fact, a turning point not just for Paul Smith but for printed textiles, because printed shirts had not been popular for many years. This was 1982 or 3 or 4 and then suddenly this shirt popularised print again. Until then, the factory I was working with, one of the few in world that can print photographs well onto fabric, was on a four-day week. After this shirt, the factory became so busy it changed to 24-hour days.

Here's another strange thing I saw: a toilet on a staircase – with a banister on it. I can't remember which chapel or which museum it's in, but this image leads to a decision I made about show invitations. We all receive so much junk mail all the time, including invitations to many, many things. So of course you want to make sure your invite is more interesting than the rest when it is seen by your own particular clientèle. When you're a young designer starting out, you wonder why anyone might keep your invitation and not throw it straight in the bin. So why not make something that's a bit unusual? This brings us to the photograph I took in 1984 of some kids in Japan. I was the first foreign person they'd ever seen. Later than this I asked Glen Baxter to draw an invite for us, which was in the early days of Glen Baxter – he wanted a suit and I needed an invite so we made a deal. This 'Donkey with the Hot Head' is in Karnac, Egypt.

These early days were so important. We have become so 'graphicked out' – even advertising images on a parking meter, or on the collar of a cricketer's jersey. Everything is full of graphics, everywhere. Everything has something written on it. And so I think that things that make you smile – photography, for example – must have a place in the future because it's so much more personal.

The next set of photographs I took while waiting for Pauline to come out of church in the tiny Italian village of Domazzano, where about 30 people live who come to church in their cars. I was early to pick up Pauline and so I took photographs of the funny and strange things people had hanging from their rear-view mirrors. This was part of the inspiration for a little cycling shirt invitation card made out of car air-fresheners.

Here is evidence of a man who's job it is to get rid of free newspapers. This is just one street. See how creative and determined he is to get rid of all his newspapers in whatever way he can.

Wrong things in the wrong places inspire window dressing here in the shop in Covent Garden. Putting things that are completely wrong in the window and also taking things that make you smile as well. For instance, I bought six bottles of water in Pisa from the supermarket and, completely by chance, all six of them were leaning – the bottoms of the bottles had a problem and they could not stand straight. From the same supermarket, the famous waving bottle opener, which is also broken. Near the same church in Domazzano, which I mentioned earlier, a man has made a little house for his tractor, but he put wheels on his house so he could move either the tractor or the house. Nearby, a tree, growing on the top of a wall.

In central Tokyo, you're not allowed to own a car unless you can prove you can park it somewhere. So this house is almost incidental and is pushed at the back of the cars and the motor bike. They have crammed something that is too big into a space that is too small. That might suggest, for example, that I could try to put a huge Christmas tree in a tiny shop window, playing with scale. Or you can mix the old with the new, like this image from Shanghai: an old Mao Tse Tung statue but with a modern

communication tower. Like a Tom Dixon chair next to a Chippendale chair, or a modern

painting in a traditional environment.

Serial imagery can be a powerful tool, too. This poster of Cheryl Crow looks good

and strong on its own, but see how strong it looks  when it's

presented as a repeated image. Postage stamps on an envelope can have the same effect.

I can use this device in my shops too, say on a top shelf I could display ten orange shirts,

which would look stronger and more positive than just one orange shirt, one blue shirt and

one green shirt. The repeated image has often been used to great effect in my shop windows.

Sometimes people take things passionately into their own hands. This is an advertisement

for Croft's Original, an English drink, and the model is obviously in quite a low-cut dress.

 Some people were so offended by it that they wanted to get rid of it. In the

next Croft Original advertisement, the décolletage is gone.

In Notting Hill Gate there are apartments called Archer House, and

another called Ledbury House, and the third one is called Denbigh House. But not after the

workmen have been at it: Denbigh House has become 'De Big House'.

Simply getting rid of the 'h' and 'n' turned it into something that makes you smile.

And here, 'No Parking' has become 'Rap King'.  This danger sign

hangs off the side of the electricity track, so it's fantastic – it has become 'Danger Mouse'.

This sign, in South Africa, simply says, 'Penguins on parking area,

check under your vehicle before departing'. The wrong thing in the wrong place! Like the

zebra in the wrong colours. This sign should say 'Dangerous Road' or something, but it has

penguins on it. I once saw an entryphone that said 'Please Knock' on it, and a

stolen cart from a railway station, which someone had locked up because they didn't want

anybody to steal it. Amazing.

I once had to give a talk for an international conference in Florence, where the

bosses of Prada, Gucci and Louis Vuitton were all speaking too. All the way through the

conference they kept referring to the 'consumer', with charts and graphs. So I gave my little

talk, and showed them a lot of these photographs, and said that I think we all sometimes

forget that, at the end of the day, what we in the fashion business do is about trading. Trade

has sponsored, in Florence, for example, much of the art and architecture too. And we

mustn't forget that we, too, 'Mr Prada', are all consumers, whether we buy a boat or a meal

or whatever, in so many different places. We should not think of shops as just chic shops.

Trading goes on all the time, everywhere. With a little stall, a trader might try so hard to make it special and different. Like this fabric shop.  When you purchase something, there are shouts and an invoice book comes down through a hole in the ceiling. They have so little space, the men who do the accounts work in the attic.

We can learn a great deal from the way that people trade who don't have much money or resources. For instance, although many people don't like the boys in Florence who hawk around sunglasses and bags, they are very clever. They used to lay their goods out on a piece of fabric on the ground. But when the police came to move them along, it took too long for them to gather up all their things. Ingeniously, they now use an old television box or a fridge box as their mobile shop. They have their shop in their hands. It has two handles, on the left and right. And as soon as the police are not looking, then these boxes become instant shops. So clever.

These people earn a living from a shop about four feet long by three feet deep, in the front window of the house where they live.  And this is in Antigua, where you're not allowed to sell things on the beach. But this is a shop. When nobody's looking, her shop turns into reality – so she undoes her shop and there suddenly you have a T-shirt for sale.

In my shops I try to get the balance right between cleverness and commerciality, in a world which is full of too many clothes. I try to make my shops more interesting by including things that are not clothes. For instance, I sold the first Dyson Cyclone cleaner – this is not the first one – when there were none available in Britain at all. They were sold only in Japan, the lilac and pink one.

I bought 50 Dyson cleaners for a men's clothes shop, and sold all 50. I like the idea of introducing other things into a clothes shop to make my shops more interesting than other people's shops. I try to have a shop where you don't need a stiff drink and a new hairdo to walk in the door, where you can find something that grabs your attention and helps you relax within the shop. In the Tokyo shop we sold old Vespas and old Lambretta scooters. We sold vinyl LPs and old fabric books, and a lot of other things much more obscure than that. In our shops in Paris, Milan, New York and London we sell old magazines, memorabilia, kitsch souvenirs, great old books and much more.

Adding a sense of humour to the shop also helps to get the balance right. There are *trompe l'oeil* paintings in our main Tokyo shop and in our Paris shop. We painted bank notes on the floors, but had to put a big six-inch nail into them because so many people were caught on their knees pretending to fix their shoelace but in fact trying to pick up the money, thinking that it was real.

Adding things like stamps in the changing rooms of one shop helps to make it different from all the others, something we try to do in Japan, where we have so many shops. In another shop, even the open and closed sign is hand-made, hand-painted. You get, at most, about 15 to 20 seconds of a person's attention when they walk by your shop. If you can create an attention-grabbing window dressing idea, you might encourage someone to visit your shop, especially if you add a sense of humour to it. Here, the man on the right is choosing a Christmas gift for the man on the extreme right, the white-haired man. A razor.

This is a ventriloquist's dummy. Obviously the ventriloquist spends a lot of time with the dummy, so the suggestion here is that maybe the ventriloquist has bad breath. So out of the left hand corner, here's an arm coming in with some Listerine for his breath, but at the same time we're promoting a watch, a cufflink, a shirt and a suit.

Often it's a case of trying to be brave enough to show things in a very minimal way. For instance, this is a spectacles window. Each day the window used to be changed, so that one day the man on the right won, and the next day the man on the left won. So when people going to work walked by there was always a little quirk that they could notice. This is an example of one of the reasons I have a successful business in Japan, and I am going to tell you why there's a picture of a rubber chicken on the back of my business card.

Through visual humour I've managed to succeed in places like Japan, where communication through language can be a big problem. Communication through humour or through some visual aid can be very successful. Just by bringing a rubber chicken out from your briefcase, you get everybody to curl up with laughter, and then, eventually, they don't forget you. So it's humour, humour. And this is just … stuff, like a box that for some reason has 'Helicopter' written on it.

This is the next section. Several years ago I had to give a lecture for people like Alexandra Shulman, the boss of British *Vogue*, and Nick Logan from *The Face* and *Arena*, for an organisation concerned with publishers and editors. They asked me to make some constructive criticisms of the magazine world, which was pretty difficult to do, seeing as there were so many VIPs in the audience, and also they were the people that gave me a lot of press. So I started off by observing that everything looks the same on the newstand, and it is a big problem because right now, everybody's looking at naked girls on the front cover. They just all look the same. I said I had decided to look at how other people solve problems when they all have an interest in the same product, and have to work out how to sell their product better than anyone else.

So I walked down to Soho, in London, to Berwick Street market, and there's just

fruit and vegetables, all sold in one street, and everybody's got the same chance of selling

their product. So I looked at one stall, and it's very untidy, and that's his way of doing it,

then I looked at another stall, and it's extremely neat and tidy. Then I started to concentrate

on one product – it could be shirts, it could be cameras but it happened to be tomatoes.

So I started looking at ways people sell tomatoes – and you get tidy tomatoes, and

you get untidy tomatoes, and then you get … tomatoes with stalks!

Now somebody's found the way, so suddenly you've got tomatoes still on the vine,

sitting on tissue paper, and presumably most of us would think, 'Well, you know, they look

nice, and I'm sure these must be fresher, or more special', and it's an example of how there's

always a way to make your product, even though it's the same product that everybody else has

got, more special, more interesting. Even in the case of a market, they can have display, even

in a market. And then I went on to talk about how magazine covers used to look, and how

brave magazines once were and how inventive they were in the past. And how they

didn't all look the same, then.

This one's from 1959, for instance, a 1959 cut out which is so modern.

I was just looking at the way things used to be, and how they are now. And talking about the

power of these covers and how beautiful they are, and how boring the

magazines have got now – because of it all being to do with how many readers there are,

which tells you how much you can charge for advertising. And how the greed of today's world

is the killer of creativity, and how – look at this spread from 1948 for instance

– it's just so sad that this level of creativity is just not happening. Look at how the copy here

is put at an angle and the photography's put at an angle – 1935 – fantastic,

it's so brave and so interesting. And then just looking at Alexey Brodovitch's work in the late

1950s, working for *Harper's Bazaar* in America. With his publishers, he insisted that some of

the money from his budget should actually be put into employing young students or young

people, or into working with colleges.

So six of his 50 pages would be to do with experimental stuff, and with using the

work of young people in a different way. Young Andy Warhol and Richard Avedon together

on one page, in 1959 or 1958. The key point is that Brodovitch insisted on

all this. My point to the publishers was … look, you're all making, say, £2 million a year,

£1 million a year, why don't you just be brave enough to talk to your shareholders about putting a certain, relatively small figure on one side? You could use it to start a new

magazine in some way, which might only have a very small circulation, but might be the

new big winner, or to give six or eight or ten pages over, within your magazine, either loose

or bound, on or within the magazine, for new people to work with. Or to work in a more

lateral way, or in a more youthful way, which is what Brodovitch did. Out of this, you may

get the work of people like Avedon. What was their reaction to that? Well … shareholders,

circulation, money. Sad, but true.

This bit now is more self promotional, because it's just talking about Westbourne

House, my shop in Notting Hill Gate, and it's coming towards the end of

my talk. In my own case, I invested £2 million into a house in a residential area, which is

a statement against the blandness of the way that all the big corporations are going. So it's

against Bond Street, it's against Sloane Street, it's against Madison Avenue. It's saying

you still can be different, you still can find a way to be more individual, even though

you're a big company.

So, taking a traditional house which was built in 1851, but which has a very modern

interior in it – we've kept the outside completely classical, and we've built a glass staircase

inside, with very personal pictures on the wall to give it a private house feeling.

There are six rooms in the house, each with its own feeling, its own atmosphere, where, because the rooms are small, you feel conversations can take place. The feeling is that these are family portraits on the wall, which are obviously only for display, and this room is a dining room – so there's a dining table, with the top cut out for display, and a chandelier, but it's in bright blue flocking, so it's not shiny gold. And there are other tables covered in velvet, there are glass panels in each wall, so there's a view through to another room, without going into the room. All the fixtures have got the feeling of wardrobes, so the shop feels like a house.

The kids' room is really like a playroom, and it's called a playroom. So even kids like going shopping there. On the floor of the kids' room there's a little thing you can press with your foot – you press that down and there's a toy that wobbles, so the kids love going in there. And there are lots of toys to play with. Then we have bespoke tailoring. Some people would say that is traditional, but by putting Andy Warhol prints even in the traditional room, it's going back to the principle of the tree on the top of the wall, or the Mao and the modern communication tower – all those things.

This is almost the end of my talk, and this image shows that even something as simple as kiddies' shoelaces can be redesigned. These are ones that you just roll in your fingers and they lace up together. And what about a sewing kit, the sort you think has probably been made by a company for three generations? Thinking about how the heck can you improve a sewing kit that you find in a hotel? But someone out there managed to think of something – you're running out to dinner, your button comes off your shirt, you go to sew on your button, then you can't thread the needle because you're in a hurry, and … it's already threaded, the needle's already threaded! So even something as simple as a sewing kit, you can always improve on – you can always think of something else. And that's the end. Thank you.

brain man
interview by professor semir zeki

Zeki: Tell me … I'm a brain man, a visual brain man. In other words, I study the visual brain, which constitutes roughly a third of our brain. You are a designer, a successful designer, of a lot of different things, although mostly of clothes. So you must have hit upon some formula that attracts people, because there is no other way of achieving this sort of success. So what would that formula be? What would you say is the main key to seducing people into buying a shirt, or something else, from you?

Making people feel special, that they are buying something special, but which won't make them look silly, or make them stand out in a crowd. The clothes are not attention-seeking, but they are special, they have something distinctive – that's probably the key.

But visually, there is something that you have hit on. For example, you say somewhere that you have an interest in Matisse and the Fauves, because they dressed objects in colours that did not belong to them.

Yes, that is right. I like the unexpected. My work has been described as classic with the unexpected – or classic with a twist. I describe it as Savile Row meets Mr. Bean, personally. So it has a sense of humour, but it also has real respect for craftsmanship and for tradition.

Do you think people feel that unconsciously, or do you think they go for that knowingly?

I think that now, unfortunately, as with many designer labels, many people buy into the image of the brand, the designer, as much as the clothes themselves. But I think when they get the clothes they are always looking for the secret, that something special …

My impression about the fashion world is that there are a lot of people who are attracted by the beautiful women and handsome men who wear these clothes in the fashion shows. But they don't look at themselves sufficiently, because some people look ridiculous in these clothes.

The big difference with Paul Smith clothes is that they are real down-to-earth clothes. Somehow, a long time ago, I managed to set the seed that it would always be a down-to-earth company, and I am a down-to-earth person. Some designers have such enormous egos, they are very self-indulgent, and only want to design what they want to design. So many of the things that they show on the catwalk are ridiculous and unwearable, and are obviously there only for the photographs and just in order to draw attention to themselves.

When you design something … I am told that you don't ever draw?

No, I never had any formal training.

I see, so it is a concept that comes into your mind?

Yes, that's why I work in this very junky way. I just write down things on pieces of paper – it could be butterfly wings, or a postman's pocket, or Matisse colours, or some reference to a Titian painting, or a sweet wrapper from the street, anything. I keep getting these things together, and I have these little orange notebooks, where I keep all this stuff – they are around here somewhere …

Do you think to yourself, 'I now need to design a shirt', for example?

No, never.

So you wait for the inspiration?

No … yes … but it's always there. Every day, I get ideas, masses of ideas, every day. The hardest thing is I lose them sometimes, because I keep them in my trouser pockets, and they go to be washed, things like that.

I do the same! So when you try things out, do you think of Mr Average?

No, I never think of anybody, or fashion trends …

But suppose someone were to walk into this room, right now, and you sensed that this person had some pretensions to being well dressed. Would you say to yourself, 'I can dress him better than that'?

Sorry not to be more clear about this, but I never over-analyse anything, I don't care how people dress at all. I think people should dress to suit their personality, and if they want to dress in some Paul Smith and some of their dad's old clothes, that's fine. If they want to dress in all Paul Smith that's fine too. If they just want to dress in anything, that's fine.

Do you never think, 'that's an ugly suit he's wearing'?

No, not really … maybe sometimes, but it would have to be pretty ugly. You see, the reason I am sitting here talking to you today, is because of my father, and my wife. My father's personality was lovely and easy, and he was easy to talk to and quite a funny person. And Pauline I met when I was 21 and a shop assistant, and she was a trained fashion designer, and kept saying, 'You've got great ideas, you have got so many brilliant ideas, you should open your own shop'. And then, eventually, I saved £600 and opened my own 'room'. It wasn't really a shop. And then Pauline started literally to make things for this shop, from ideas that we both had together – for many years they were mostly her ideas – the early Paul Smith

collections were all designed by her, not by me at all. Slowly, I learned my trade from her, not in a formal way, but in a learning-by-doing way. It was a parallel effort. It was learning to be a shop keeper, learning to be a lover, learning to be a step-father – because she had two sons – and learning to be a designer. All in parallel. And we never, at any point, ever, sat down and said, 'Let's have a fashion business, and let's have our own collection, and let it be like this'. It just all rolled along.

Because it was going from success to success?

No, it developed because there were always lots of lovely ideas, and luckily somebody out there liked them. There was never, ever, a business plan.

I understand that. But I am also interested in the fact, which you are being quite reticent about, that you have unlocked a secret. You may not even be aware of it yourself, but a lot of people have found themselves attracted to the secret you have unlocked. What do you think that secret is? You say to me one thing – that you have taught people to be themselves. That is a very

important lesson in terms of fashion, because, as I think I have told you, I have been to see the clothes at Versace fashion shows, and the clothes are great, really great. But everyone there is chosen for being extremely beautiful. And what suits Naomi Campbell does not suit the average woman. So there is something else that you have unlocked, something that is common to all people. So … how many people, roughly, do you reckon, buy something from your shops around the world? A million?

Over a million.

That's a hefty whack.

We shift a million items out of the Nottingham warehouse, and then in Japan we sell 90,000 suits a year, a quarter of a million shirts a year, so … I wonder whether it is because I didn't have any formal training, so I didn't really try to be a designer. I think being called a designer is a burden for a lot of people. In one of my early jobs, I remember just coming up with the idea of a simple white shirt, and my boss saying, 'Well, it's just a simple white shirt'. And I said, 'Yes, but it has a soft collar that's smaller

than the ones that are around at the moment; it has mother-of-pearl buttons, 22 stitches to the inch, deep armholes and it's in sea-island cotton. It's a simple shirt, but it's a very nice simple white shirt.' And I think probably because of my naivety, because I didn't know about design as such, I just nudged things, rather than trying to come up with a nine-armed jacket, or something shocking and attention-seeking. So some of my early successes were just things like taking a traditional Prince of Wales check and putting the 'wrong' colour overcheck in it, or a purple lining, or the 'wrong' blue cuff on a green shirt.

Wrong?

Well, it wasn't what was normally accepted. It might be a Bengal striped shirt in maroon and white, and I would put a blue-and-white striped cuff on it — maybe only because I couldn't think what else to do — as opposed to drawing a pocket with six pleats in it, because I didn't know how to do that.

Look at a designer like Lanvin, very classical, very sedate. It may suit a certain type, not of this age any more, the upper-bourgeoisie of yester-year type.

Yes, there you are literally buying for the cachet of the label, that means something to you.

Chanel is one of the designers of the past whom I admire. She unlocked one or two secrets. One secret which we know she unlocked, is that she got rid of girdles and things that made people uncomfortable. And on top of that, she came up with a design that can look elegant. Chanel suits, even today, I think look elegant, on a lot of women. Do you agree?

Yes, absolutely, and of course she was the pioneer of big Oxford bag trousers. And the Chanel suit was very distinctive, because it was in bouclé, it was a certain length, and she had the idea of the chain in the back of the jacket, which holds it down and makes it always look elegant. ... I didn't know I had done that, unlocked something.

You have, there is no question about it. The interesting thing for me as a physiologist is to understand what it is. I consider artists and designers to be, in a sense, neurologists. You study the brain, as I do, but with a different method. And your measure of success is something different. Your measure would be sales. If you found you were not selling anything, you would rethink your designs, or you would decide to jack the whole thing in. But the fact is, you have been rewarded.

The person who was a designer for Chanel, Karl Lagerfeld, he sells some designs which are not commercial. And some designs of Alexander McQueen, which I have seen in pictures — I have never been to one of his shows — are rather outlandish; hats with fruits and things, they are so theatrical — how many of these things can he actually sell? There must be a reason in his head for that. He must sell almost none, but what happens is that through attention-seeking fashion shows he has built up an interest and confidence in certain buyers who know that what he shows on the catwalk is different from what he shows in the showroom. And as you probably know, he now has a partnership with Gucci, so they obviously think he can be commercially successful.

Do you have fashion shows?

Yes, we just had one for men, in Paris, on 1 July, which was the Spring 2002 collection. The women's one is in London, in September. But they are all wearable clothes.

Do you find it easier to design for men or for women?

Men, by far. Because that is what I started with, and I really understand it. Although I understand women's design better now, it's not just about clothes, it's about many, many other things. It's about what you are trying to say, about the look of the woman, the hair, the makeup, the type of woman she is ... it changes fast, and is a demanding area of fashion. There is not so much loyalty from the customers; men, if they like

you, will stay with you for a long time.

What is it that appeals to men about your clothes? What sort of age group do you appeal to?

I think my biggest achievement is that in the early 1980s I got the average British male to understand that it was fine to enjoy clothes, it wasn't a feminine thing, and it was okay.

You think they didn't understand this?

I am talking about the general public. In the 1960s there were outlandish hippies, in the 1970s and early 1980s there was power dressing. But with Paul Smith, especially in the early 1980s, when I got started properly in the financial area, people in more serious businesses – newspapers, finance – bought my things. Because I only nudged things, just did little things to clothes, by perhaps changing the colour slightly, because I didn't have the confidence to do anything more outlandish, and because I am just a regular guy, other regular guys thought it was okay to wear Paul Smith. Then you could start to think about how you looked, and it wasn't considered a problem. That was an interesting achievement.

People were maybe psychologically afraid, before you pointed out to them that they could do these things?

Yes, and there was peer group pressure. People walking into an office in a brightly coloured tie would just get laughed at. But eventually, because of people like me – and I certainly wasn't alone in this – it just became okay, not a problem, to wear, say, a lemon-coloured sweater. And also travel helped a lot. On package holidays people would see that very regular Spanish or Italian or French males could wear a bright coloured sweater, and it was okay. And the other thing, to answer your question, the other thing I am really thrilled about, is the fact that we sell to 16-year-olds and 60-year-olds. We sell to people in banking, well-known artists, architects, and also to students, young men who are buying their first suit, rock-stars – an amazing range. I find that most exciting.

If I were to come to you tomorrow, and ask you to dress me, because I wanted to look really elegant and dashing, would you have a concept of how you would go about it?

Absolutely. There would be no problem about that.

So you would have a well-formed concept in your brain?

The first thing is, through discussion, over a cup of coffee, to find out what you are really like, as a human being. I had one very amusing experience, when I had a phone call from a record company saying, 'We have got five urchins, and £5,000, and we would like you to dress them'. And they later became a very famous group. I invited them here, and we had coffee and croissants, and through talking to them I picked up that the character of one of them was quite classical; the way he held himself, and the way he was, he would suit something pretty simple. Another guy, the keyboard player, the singer, was very articulate, and his hair was more wild, and I could see I could put him in more flamboyant things. If it was you, I would consider your lifestyle, your job, your shape, and work out what would suit you.

So you don't go on physique only?

Not at all, no. Although you can do a lot with the physique, you can advise people not to wear things because it will make them look shorter – wide trousers on a short man will make him look even shorter, for example.

There must be people who come to you and ask you to dress them?

Yes, mostly musicians, or actors.

And do they ever come back and say they don't like themselves in what you have chosen?

No, never. But that is because I am now experienced enough not to be arrogant, and tell people anything. You do it by discussion. Sometimes through joking.

So, what I have established now, as a physiologist, is that you have a concept in your mind, which you might develop

during a conversation with me, as to what sort of person I am, and how you would dress me. Now, if I were to say, right now, 'think of an ideal suit', would you have a clear ideal in mind?

Yes, an ideal suit is one that is not trying too hard. One that is quite simple. The width of the shoulder would not be too extreme; the size of the shoulder pad not too extreme; the proportion of the pockets average … these proportions are standard, and the result of years of experience; you can get the perfect Palladian proportion in a suit as well as in a building. So it would probably be a single-breasted suit, two or three buttons, not extreme in any way. The trousers are more of a problem, because of the waist size. Certain trousers suit different waist sizes.

Now, a diversion. While I was waiting for you, I looked at the trousers in your shop downstairs. I noted that you don't have pleated trousers here. I think that pleated trousers are a disaster, do you agree?

Well, we do practically no business with pleated trousers.

Your customers have great taste then; because pleated trousers only suit very tall, very slim people. But if you go today to Yves Saint Laurent, or Pierre Cardin, or any of the big designers, you are hard put to find trousers that are not pleated. I don't know how they have managed to push this hideous style down people's throats. I gather that Prada has stopped using pleats, too, which is good, but you have never used them?

Well, maybe at some point, but only if there was a certain look I was trying to achieve. But I think whatever success I have is due, partly, to the fact that I started as a shop assistant, and then had my own shop. This meant I learned about the balance that is required in a shop. So, if you only have a certain set of clothes in your shop, you are almost certain to have a problem on your hands, while if you have a little bit more of a variety,

then you have more chance of survival. In the very beginning, in 1970, when I started, I thought, 'I don't want the job to change me', so I only opened the shop two days a week – Friday and Saturday. I never had any compromise. I only sold clothes that I wanted to sell. Because I knew that if I tried to make a living from the shop, then the job would change me, because I would have to compromise. And that wasn't what I wanted at all. So I earned a living in various jobs from Monday to Thursday, and then had my two days of purity, which was selling what I wanted to sell. In the end, I went and started a real shop, rather than a back room, and started paying out real rent, which is when I had to allow the job to change me more than before.

I think you perhaps rather underestimate yourself, or at least your brain. Because there is not a little complexity here, in achieving something that appeals to so many people. And what we have established is that you have got away from the single design that suits everybody. Obviously, that is crazy. And the second thing we have established is that you have a concept in your mind. Which is quite, quite, interesting. You have an ideal suit, which you have to deviate from occasionally, but presumably you stick as closely as you can to this.

The word I think I have used several times is 'nudge'. The danger is shoving, pushing.

Are there any designers, any types of designers, or designs, that you specially dislike?

I don't like attention-seeking design. Stupid ideas, that can't be worn. Clothes that have unnecessary parts to them, which are too outrageous. I understand about design, about unusual design; I respect the Japanese designer, Rae Kawakubo, who has the label Comme des Garçons. Often her clothes are really crazy, but underneath it all there is always quite an interesting side to her design, and geniune craft, so I can accept that.

But often, young students, when they do their final show, really think that the only way to get noticed is to do extreme things, and I don't think that's a good thing, personally. Bare breasts, for example, have always astounded me on the catwalk. But they are presumably only there for photography. They do this all the time in the women's shows; it is very normal, but usually just for the shock value. I have done it occasionally, but only because it has seemed to fit in with the garment being worn – you know, a light fluid garment, that is quite sexy looking. But often nudity is exploited just to get attention from the press.

But is it not more attractive to have things slightly hidden?
In my opinion, yes.

There is a neurological reason for that, because your imagination can get to work.
My clothes for women … and all my clothes on the catwalk, for men and women, are all available in the shops. That's quite rare. And I think I agree with you, it comes back to my early training by Pauline; she taught me that the quality of making something, the interior, the construction, the proportion of clothes, this can all create an extremely sexy, or elegant, garment through cut alone. If you look at regimental, ceremonial clothing, for the army or navy, the cut of the trouser is amazing, so slim and so well cut. It is very high waisted, it arches in to the back, the bottom of the trouser is angled, and it is all to do with elegance, and elongating the figure. Also you will find that the armhole is very shallow, very narrow, which makes the distance from the waist to the shoulder even longer, and it is always tightly cut through the rib cage, which is an attractive part of both a man and a woman.

I agree with what you say. And what amazes me is how, for a period recently, baggy trousers were all the rage. How did that happen?
I think it's the opposite, really. Because baggy trousers really look great if you are extremely thin. You pull them in, and then it is all about what your imagination tells you is going on inside.

When you design, do you have an average person, or height, in mind?
You don't have to, but one tends to work to an industry standard, because otherwise you wouldn't sell a lot of clothes. The danger for a designer, if you are short or fat or tall, is to design clothes for yourself, because obviously that limits who will buy them.

What about cutting, and materials, and things like that? Do you choose them yourself? Do you have cutters?
Yes, cutters and the toillistes are very important. The toillistes pin the mock-ups on the stand for you, so you can see in advance how the clothes are going to look. They are very skilled people. In France, most designers are called stylists, but the toilliste is an essential ingredient there. Especially someone like Chanel, or Saint Laurent. Cut is incredibly important.

Also, how I start, I try to work around a theme for each collection. I know at the end of the day it is only about a customer coming in and buying a shirt, so they couldn't care two hoots about your theme, really. But by having a theme, you can draw on your imagination to create all aspects of the theme. And if you have assistant designers it's a good way of describing what you want.

So can you give me an example of a theme? I can see it is important, to help in organising things.
I have had collections with funny names. 'Poet with a Few Bob', 'Dandy Meets Rock 'n Roll'. The Spring/Summer 2002 collection is called 'Rebel Son'. Collections always have themes, and as you have identified, I do have a certain way of thinking, which probably repeats itself, so it's always a version of the same way. 'Dandy Meets Rock 'n Roll' was a boy who thinks a lot about how he dresses. He is not embarrassed to get up in the morning and think about his clothes. He might enjoy the

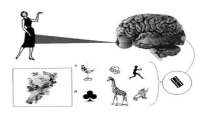

history of someone like Cecil Beaton or Oscar Wilde in terms of 'dandiness', but he is a bit more rock 'n roll than that, a bit more 'fuck you', so he would have a very ripped pair of jeans with a very elegant jacket. He is a rebellious sort of boy, I suppose. 'Poet with a Few Bob' was a dreamy sort of character, someone like Van Morrison, perhaps. Or he could have been a poet laureate, like Cecil Day Lewis. He could have been living in Ireland, and limited in what he can buy, so he will buy an Arran sweater, or some Donegal tweed, but on his trips to London, he will pick up a bit of fashion, which he will mix with his romantic corduroy trousers. Or he might have a girlfriend who knits his sweaters. He's a bit scruffy, so the clothes were washed, but not ironed.

So the unifying theme in your given concept is the character of the person, rather than the physique?
Yes.

This is interesting, most unusual. I would have thought that most designers would go straight for the physique. And basically, the truth is that most of us are not very good looking. There is a very important secret, here, that other designers, I don't think …
That's the point. If you look at, say, Prada, Gucci, Saint Laurent, now under their new ownership – well Gucci and Saint Laurent are – they are going for a big push of change; but basically, their man is always sexy, slim.

There is a great difficulty with that. For example, whenever I go to somewhere like Ermenegildo Zegna, or to Hugo Boss, I invariably come out after five minutes, because they say to me – when I have tried one jacket, and found it too long – 'All our jackets are this long'. Basically they are saying they have nothing for me.
We did a photographic campaign, with David Bailey, and chose ordinary people as models; a big person, a slim person, a Rastafarian, an Indian boy, an interior designer, a rugby player. Because of that whole point. I am interested in just people, and honestly don't over-analyse anything.

But you do analyse. You say you don't – artists are always denying what they do – but you have a whole concept of people, of what they might feel like.
Maybe I do analyse a lot. Maybe I just treat it in a throw-away manner.

I think you may throw some things out, but you distil some things out, and use that in your designs. Last weekend, in Paris, you gave a talk about your 'Rebel Son' collection. 'Rebel Son' was about a rich, aristocratic Argentinian boy, who pillaged his family home – taking the curtains, stuff from his father's wardrobe – to deconstruct, recut and reassemble into clothes to suit his own style. You used the words, 'When I went there, in my mind', when you were thinking about this character. You even thought about the house he lived in.
And I've never even been to Argentina!

And one of the jackets in the collection is made from a print of an illustration of an Argentinian home in the hills, with trees and so on. This is fascinating. Is this the substitute for working out ideas with a pencil line, on paper, like most designers?
Well, yes, and that is definitely what I will be doing on my holiday, during the next few weeks, when I will be designing Autumn/Winter 2002. The week I come back, we have a design meeting in Nottingham, with two assistant designers. They will be wanting the idea, the theme. So during my holiday in Tuscany, I'll really be somewhere else.

Can you explain how you do that, how you gather things from your travels, then get your designers to realise what you want?
Well, for example, I know a young man in Paris who introduced me to a photographer from Lithuania. We looked at his work and talked about Lithuania – about restaurants, food, the environment there – and he said he knew designers in Lithuania. And he said something that sticks in my mind. He said these Lithuanian designers just have to use whatever fabrics they can get hold of; now and again they get material from somewhere else, which they mix with their usual fabrics. And this just goes on and on in my mind, and might be the start

of something for next winter. It might not be, but immediately I am thinking of some old-fashioned striped fabric, which has always been available in Lithuania, maybe for a postman, or a heavy cloth, which they might use for army uniforms, and they suddenly then mix it with a nylon Adidas fabric, which they have managed to get 50 yards of, from somebody who has come from England. So that will get written down, and might end up being something like 'Putting the wrong fabrics together', something like that.

And do you then order the fabrics?

Yes. I do all the colour choice of the fabrics. We work very much on colour. We work around a theme, which then helps you with colour. Obviously colour is based on information as well. Because, if you have been doing well with 'bright, bright, bright' – eventually it will go 'pastel, pastel, pastel', or 'monochrome', or whatever. So it is definitely based on information. And then the theme is important. And when you have established the theme, and you are comfortable with it, you go to the fabric fairs, which are held in Italy and France twice a year, and then obviously you have this person in your head. So if I am going down the Lithuanian route, I will think of old-fashioned stripes, I'll think of maybe some tweed, and then suddenly I'll get a completely modern high-tech fabric, and I will either make the flaps of the jacket out of it, or the sleeves, or it will be a jacket that goes over tweed, or …

Do you ever get inspired … for example, I gather that Yves Saint Laurent sets himself up in Morocco, because the colours are so exciting there … do you get inspiration in this way from your immediate surroundings?

Well, as the title of this book says – you can find inspiration in everything. I just observe everything. I always have a camera, and a notebook. So, unlike Saint Laurent, who has a specific place where he finds his ideas, I could be inspired by someone I see in Notting Hill Gate, or in Rajasthan, or in Tuscany.

But you told me at the beginning that your main designs are of clothes, so your ideas are channelled into designing clothes rather than other things.

Yes, but the things I see also influence the window dressing in my shops, which is very important in Paul Smith, and how the shops look generally, as well.

Another important thing you have unlocked, which you may or may not be aware of, is that you say somewhere that you have to capture people's attention; they will look at something for about 20 seconds, no more, unless you interest them. So this is your operational window, and you have to grab people in that brief moment. There is a profound physiological truth in that. So, you have unlocked them, gained their attention, and during that brief moment, what do you do to hold their attention?

I use humour. That's what we hope to hit them with. Visual humour. Using lateral thinking, mostly, and plenty of self-confidence. For instance, there was one window … the weather had been appalling for ten weeks, and on the window, inside, there was just a post-it note, which said 'Sorry, no display, gone to the Bahamas'. And another one was … a big bouncy ball, the sort kids bounce on, in the corner of the window. No clothes in the window at all. And you look in and think, 'That's strange, no clothes?' And then you realise there's just the legs of a mannequin, a boy, just on the top of the unit, which is where

he's meant to have bounced to – only he hasn't yet bounced back. And this always, without meaning to, this is always saying something about you, about the company. In my head, they say, 'This is not your standard roll-out corporate company, your standard shop. This is a confident shop. This is a shop that makes me smile.'

And extending that, how do you attract attention to the product? Because that is a 20 second thing, isn't it?

I am not worried about that, because I think that there are so few Paul Smith shops, that the sort of people who might buy our clothes already know what we stand for.

How many Paul Smith shops are there in London?

Eleven.

Well, that's not bad!

I quite like the fact that there is no product in there. In a way, it just shows more confidence.

Before I turn to women – if I were to go downstairs with you, and try something on which you thought did not suit me, would you tell me?

Yes. And so would the staff. They are always told that the most important person is not me, but the customer. It is important to have sales, but it is not the vital ingredient. The vital ingredient is that the customer comes back, that they have a long life with us.

Do you have a concept of the nicest dress on a woman?

Probably, just a little black dress. Something very simple. Black respects the form very well, because it is so solid. And it would be really, really simple. When I first started to design for women – I resisted for ten years, and then eventually gave in – I really thought I could just … the girls kept saying to me, 'just make what you make for men, but smaller'. And so we made suits, and shirts and sweaters, and then of course they said they needed a dress, or a skirt, and then it turned into me getting quite scared about doing it. I got what I called a 'blender head' problem. My head felt like a food blender. And I was really quite scared. I went to see my doctor, who is a friend. He said I was taking in too much information, too many opinions, and I was in a no-win situation. Others were winning, but I wasn't winning because I was not good at being confrontational; so he taught me to balance situations out more, to make things more even, more of a 'win-win' situation. And when I learned that, I found I could approach women's wear better, with more confidence. I could say 'This is what I am doing', with confidence. It took about two years to work it out.

How many years ago is it that you started designing clothes for women?

About eight years ago, I think. I'm not sure exactly. So after I had been designing for men for about 22 years.

Women are infinitely more complicated to design for, I imagine. I agree with you, that a simple black dress is absolutely wonderful for women – do you agree that they are more complicated to design for?

A lot more, because shape, of course, is one thing. Lifestyle, attitude, just associated things, like you have to be more clear who you are trying to sell to, with women. You have to know. My brief in my head, was girlfriend, wife, lover, of my more creative male Paul Smith customer. And that turned out to be pretty true, actually. So … intelligent, maybe a mum, or

an architect and a mum, or a writer, or a singer, but pretty creative. So quite healthy looking, quite clean looking.

So you had a concept in your mind?

Yes, I had to, there. Because I was lost, otherwise.

So these ultra-thin women would not be at all your …

Well, thin women happen to be what we have to use … we use professional models in the shows because they are great clothes hangers, the clothes look great on a really slim girl, but our clothes are not just for … well, they are for slender girls …

Well, maybe slender, but there are those ultra-ultra-slim girls. I don't know whether the fashion is still for those.

Yes, it is the fashion still. But real girls are not all like that. Paul Smith clothes are for slim girls, though, not for big girls, unfortunately – for all sorts of boring practical reasons, minimum production runs, that sort of thing. You just have to make a decision; 'My type of girl is this type …'.

But one might say that your type of girl is more representative than most of the girls you see at the catwalk shows.

Yes, and we make simple sweaters, simple blue jeans, simple corduroy trousers, as well as the more luxurious silk, chiffon, couture fabrics. Sandra Hill, my design director on the womens collections, and I – and the whole womens team, in fact – work very hard you know!

insert
the bunny
a paul smith comic book

ambassador*

*Statements by Paul Smith edited from previously published texts, articles or interviews, 1990–2001.

My job is a bit like those jugglers that spin plates on poles. Keeping them all spinning perfectly is difficult. There is always one which starts to wobble when you are designing 19 collections a year, have more than 250 shops, 450 staff and are the chairman of the company.

People in creative industries have to find new ways to innovate. Twenty years ago it was impossible to get an espresso coffee outside London. Today everything is 'good'. The challenge now is to be better than that, more interesting than 'good'.

You can't take anything for granted, especially in the fashion industry. You are only as good as the clothes you produce today. You can't rest on your laurels. I'm still very critical of myself and of the work I do. I get excited by new collections and by a fashion show that I find that we've got right, but I don't like them all. I get quite upset if I feel we're not good enough, and it's hard to make sure that every collection you do is 100 per cent the best, because we're doing so much.

Fashion does a job. I don't think it's art and I think it's massively over-rated by the people in it. It's not over-rated as a creator of jobs, and as an industry, and designers are important, and clothes *do* do a job: clothes can make you sexy or important or aggressive. But it's not like we're sewing arms back on people or anything.

Photo: Platon, New York, 1999.

The reason I've been successful is because I've just got on and packed boxes, and know that VAT means Value Added Tax not vodka and tonic. I've sold on the shop floor, I've typed invoices. At some point I've done everything, and I've always kept my head above water financially. Nevertheless, I'm extremely nervous about becoming a businessman and not a designer.

I would never say our clothes are cheap, but I balk when people tell me they're expensive. Compared to what? If you look at other fashion houses who use fabric from the same suppliers – Armani, et al – we're actually cheaper because we take lower profit margins at the wholesale level and we don't have their grand showrooms and advertising budgets.

And it's wrong to compare us with Next and others. Out of the 30 or so countries we deal with, Britain's the only one where the high street is dominated by price-cutting chains. On the continent we deal with small shops, often family-owned.

Our collection is unconventional in both size and depth. Quantity is the key to keeping costs down and we have shorter runs than most – we might produce a run of 500 sweaters, while Marks & Spencer wouldn't make fewer than perhaps 20,000. We want to make it unlikely that you'll go into a pub or club and meet someone wearing the same thing.

We compensate by having a much wider range than other designers – maybe 1,600 rather than 600 items in a collection. That means almost three times as many paper patterns in graded sizes. Then there are the detailed specifications – colour, buttons, linings – all multiplied 1,600 times. It becomes like an army manoeuvre.

We probably suffer less from an increase in variable costs than most businesses – although we do get affected when the pound drops or cashmere prices go through the roof. Our clothes are not price-sensitive like other commodities, in the sense that sales would not drop if a suit cost £10 more.

Preparing a collection is an incredibly long and expensive process and is one of the main reasons why fashion companies go under. I start work on a Spring collection in February of the preceding year, drawing up the overall look of the collection, picking the colour themes and visiting mills to supply and develop the unique fabrics we need – a one-off print or stripe. We want to be leaders, not followers, so that means doing something subtly different, even with a standard navy blue wool.

By May we have the sample metres made up into mock-ups and samples are then made for the selling shows. We have our own show-rooms in Milan, Paris, London and Tokyo and stage our own shows in Paris and London. It's at this time that the wholesale orders are placed, and once they are collated and fabric bought, production will start in June or July. The treadmill never stops. By this time I'll already be working on the next season's collection.

The shops themselves don't set targets for achieving a fixed sales return per square foot. Where you might expect to find an extra rack squeezed into another shop, you're just as likely to find a sofa, moped or painting in one of mine. A lot of the things don't turn into money directly, but they give people a special feeling about the place, which pays off in the end.

The other thing we do is throw in a range of inexpensive items – perhaps something as daft as a toothbrush – so that we end up with very few people actually walking out without buying anything. It encourages them to come back another time when they may buy some clothes.

Financially we're conservative. There was a time when we could have thought about going public, but we never aspired to it. We ploughed money back into the business in the form of bricks and mortar – buying our freeholds in Covent Garden and in Nottingham – which have made banks comfortable about dealing with us when we need short-term finance.

We've also found the value of treating wholesale customers well during a recession. We've never forced anybody to take a certain amount of stock, which some of our rivals do. The strange thing is, it has all worked.

Recession blights many companies in the fashion business, but we've always come through with sales rising. We've never had a grand master plan dreamed up in some ivory tower. The shops and wholesale operation just grew and grew.

We do have a very focused marketing strategy – we need to, with retail turnover of about £315m worldwide. But we still manage to keep it fairly light-hearted.

When the orders are actually shipped, cash-flow is at its weakest and this is when some houses get stretched to busting point. All the money has gone out on hotels, flights, zips, buttons, fabrics and shipping. The actual production of clothes – cut, make and trim – is traditionally paid for in seven days. But not a penny has come in from wholesale clients around the world. You need credit controllers who can say 'pay up please' in 30 languages. We are incredibly lucky to have the retailing side. Give or take seasonal variations, it is a regular earner for us, flattening the mountains and valleys of the cash-flow throughout the year. Retailing may appear to others as an inspired move on our part, but we did it the other way round. I started with a shop, then designed a small collection to sell in it. Only then did I become conscious of how important it was for cash-flow.

Photo: Marc Hom, New York, 1998.

The hard fact remains: most fashion business is done abroad. The world's press and buyers attend the French and Italian collections, affording exhibitors the opportunity of international press coverage and international sales; what more could one ask? Our top womenswear designers could, and should, choose to support London Fashion Week, but when London is the third choice on the fashion map after Milan and Paris, they often choose to go abroad.

The British public are becoming increasingly aware that British fashion designers, in order to achieve international recognition, are having to cross the Channel to do so. Our ideas are exported, too, often with no gain for ourselves. For decades now, British youth culture has produced some of the most extraordinary fashion statements, yet these ideas are invariably plagiarised and watered down by our European cousins. And who can blame them? If British industry is unwilling to develop the wealth of available talent, then why should we criticise others for ripping them off?

British design is capable of making the ordinary extraordinary, but a failure to invest in product development has forced many British designers to leave Britain. Paradoxically, Britain is a nation committed to design education. With thousands of students enrolled on hundreds of design-led courses, Britain is widely regarded as having the largest, most successful training system in the world. The wealth of talent that emerges, however, is often snapped up by the international commercial giants. Bang & Olufsen (Danish), Tefal (French), Electrolux (Swedish) and Sony (Japanese) *all* employ British designers at the highest level. And in the fashion world the same thing applies. For the past few years Britain has also had a trade deficit in office furniture, an area where it has traditionally been strong. But what do we find? British design is leading the world. Herman Miller (US), Vitra (Germany), Akaba (Spain), Knoll International (US), Facit (Sweden) and Syrma (Italy) all employ British designers. The portfolio of British designers who have had top-selling products manufactured abroad and imported back to Britain reads like a Who's Who? of design.

In 1992 I declined my nomination as British Designer of the Year. My main reason for turning down this award was to try and highlight the problems of the British fashion industry. I see no advantage in continued self-congratulatory events when our own design industry is so insignificant in world terms.

And as for the design values we do appreciate, they are hardly cutting edge. You only have to look at the world of retail to see this. On the one hand we seem intent on exploiting the heritage industry – turning once thriving mill towns into post-modern shopping centres – while on the other we're turning our market towns into homogenised malls. Walk down any high street in Britain and you could, in fact, be walking down any high street in Britain. British Home Stores, Next, Tesco, HMV and all the rest – the shop fronts, the interiors and often even the products themselves are uniform from Glasgow to Gloucester.

During the 1980s the high street became an embarrassment. In the 1960s, when Terence Conran started Habitat, he saw the high street as a very boring place indeed, and the changes he helped initiate were highly exciting. But 20 years later things had come full circle, and the high street had ended up being just as predictable as it was in the 1960s. The retail revolution imploded, and rent structures became so prohibitive that the local butchers, chemist, florists and bakers who once gave cities their own unique identity are now virtually extinct. We used to be a nation of shopkeepers, whereas now we are little but a theme park without a theme.

Unless more British manufacturers start responding to changes in design technology, British design will continue to farm out production to Italy and France. Most British clothing manufacturers refuse to produce short runs of garments, and as a result many designers are forced to produce their collections abroad. Wouldn't it be better to have a truly integrated industry where design and manufacturing ideas could be developed through mutually beneficial business partnerships?

The time has come for Britain to realise the export potential of good design. To concentrate solely on the home market is crazy. My home market constitutes only about 25–30% of my turnover. Only through persuasion, enthusiasm and the promise of a limitless future was I able to ensure the support of a handful of manufacturers when I began 30 years ago. I was fortunate in developing business relations with people who understood the necessity for originality in the market place. Sadly, hundreds of British mills and factories have since closed down, unable to compete with the cheap imports that flooded the market in the 1970s.

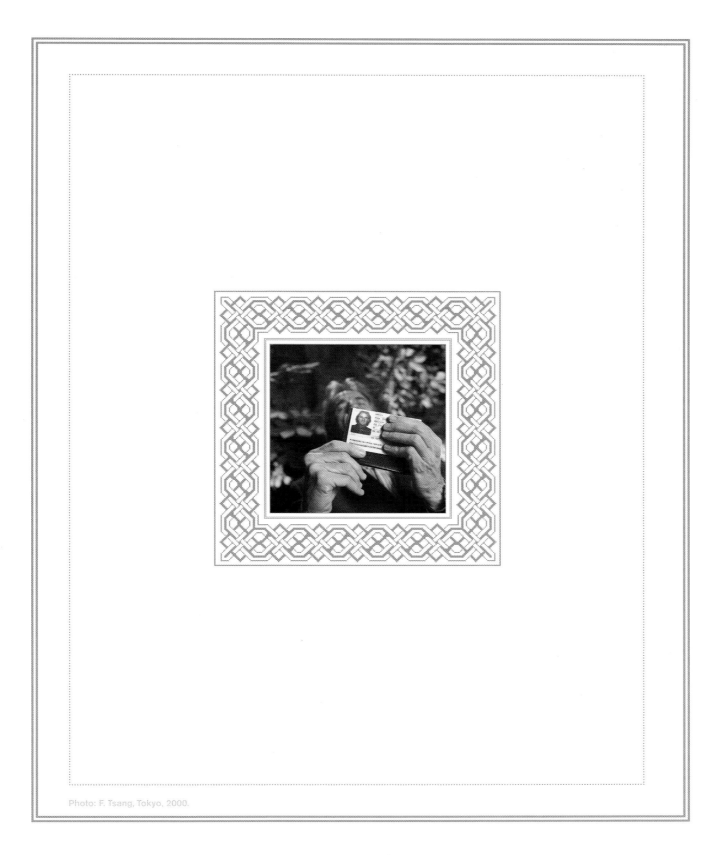

⌘ shop windows ⌘

Humour is important in my shop windows, even if there aren't any Paul Smith clothes in the display. Sometimes they change daily. And that means *all* my shop windows, from New York to Hong Kong. You've got to catch people's attention. They are as important as my catwalk shows in London and Paris.

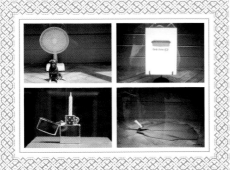

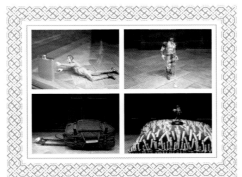

Clockwise from top left:
Fan and dog figure * Hot dog T-shirt * Paul Smith lighter and
birthday candle * Sleeveless pullover and marker pen

Hip flask and action figure * Necklace and action figure * Traveller
bag and toy truck * Matchstick photo-print cusion and action figure
holding a pipe

Monkey cufflinks and gorilla figure * Chilli pepper keyring and
chilli pepper * Letter socks and envelopes * Sunglasses and action
figures

Watch and bananas * Sunglasses and action figure * Shoes and
feathers * Christmas goodies and bicycle wrapped in tinsel

Opposite:
'Grrr' pendant and 'Mr T' action figure * Toothbrush and action
figure * Post-it note * Cufflinks and toy robot

MANY PEOPLE LOOK BUT THEY DO NOT SEE

I have been lucky with the press, but that is because there is a story to tell. It is very difficult for a lot of companies to find a story at all. If you are making something basic, it is difficult to ring a fashion magazine and say 'I've got a grey crew-neck'. They would say 'So what?' But if your grey crew-neck is made from silk, by hand, you may find a way through the reeds to the sea yet again. There is always some way to try. Packaging and presentation are also important, as are graphics, notepaper, the welcome of your office receptionist, pleasant well-mannered people with a good telephone technique, and, most of all, a broad outlook. When you travel around the world, you must look and see; many people look but they do not see. They are always worried about the time of their flight, that the food is weird. They should forget such things and just get on and enjoy travelling and try to learn something new.

Photo: M. Katsura, Tokyo, 1999.

Photo: Roberto Frankenberg, at Deyrolles, a taxidermist, Paris, 2001.

My problem is I don't want to slow down.

How could I? It would be a nightmare to stop. I don't
want to take someone's money and stop working; if we
were to go into business with someone else, I'd have to
stay involved or it wouldn't be worth it.

CHECKING IT OUT

Design is only good if it is linked with market research – which I call 'checking it out', seeing what is going on in the world. In other words, thinking locally. If Italy has a wealth of beautifully made suits, the chances are you will not sell too many beautifully made suits, but you might be able to sell interesting sweaters or shirts to go with them.

As in many industries, there has been an onslaught of take-overs in the world of fashion. Many companies have become motivated by the bottom line and by pleasing the shareholders; there's a danger of killing creativity. For me it's all about continuing to expand the business in a way that still keeps it very personal, with a heart.

The last 30 years have been fantastic, and although it's not always been easy it's always been fun. Which, after all, is what it's all about.

I was completely honest when I started the women's line. I said I would need three to five years, because I didn't understand this world. Also, when it started, the collection was very much about clothes for women that weren't necessarily clothes for the catwalk – that was the whole point: a nice white shirt, a suit, a jacket. It just wasn't big or mature enough, and now it is, I hope.

Apart from designing the collections, I am not keen on the world of womenswear, the falseness of it. Put your hand on your heart and tell me it's not false. It's not a real world. Many people in fashion are attentive to somebody else because they think they're going to get something out of it. So many designers forget that the customers are, in the end, the VIPs. It's like a magazine's readers: the publisher doesn't pay the writers and designers, the readers do.

I now expect to come across fake Paul Smith jeans or T-shirts from time to time. One of the most copied Paul Smith items is the logo, so if you see a large 'Paul Smith' on a T-shirt, then it's a fake. I think we've sued successfully about 120 times for that kind of thing, but I was most shocked by the completely false 'Paul Smith' shop we discovered in Bangkok, almost identical to our real shop in Floral Street. And it stood next to a completely fake 'Comme des Garçons' shop. Someone had obviously come in, taken down all the measurements and copied them exactly. We've since caught one other guy in London with a tape measure, sizing up all the fittings.

It was a lovely surprise to receive the letter from Downing Street, telling me that I was to receive a Knighthood for services to the fashion industry. It arrived in the post, with my credit card and telephone bills.

It feels good to be recognised for what I've done for fashion and design. It's also good for the industry, because fashion is sometimes treated rather flippantly. We employ a lot of people and we're a big contributor to the economy, but often this industry gets the wrong image – that it's about strange clothes and eccentric people. Not so.

Despite all this, you've got to keep your feet on the ground. That's easily the most important thing in the fashion business.

Photo: Hugh Hales-Tooke, Paris, 1991.

With mother and father. Photo: *Mr High Fashion* magazine, Nottingham, 1995.

With Pauline Denyer Smith. Photo: Joe Gaffney, London, 1991.

paul smith
by paul smith

for paul smith

Paul Smith, age 24, and Paul Smith, age 35, both athletes, Hutton-le-Hole.

Paul Smith, age 49, public house proprietor, Cheshire.

Paul Smith, age 20, chef, Cheshire.

Paul Smith, age 22, magician, Swindon.

Paul Smith, age 28, stonemason, Wakefield.

Paul Smith, age 28, telephone engineer, Enfield.

Paul Smith, age 55, drummer, Roundhay.

Paul Smith, age 27, photographer, London.

contributors

Sir Paul Smith

Paul Smith (b. 1946) is perhaps the most successful fashion designer in British history. Still independently owned, Paul Smith's clothing label has 14 shops in Britain and more than 240 shops in Japan. In 1991 he was awarded the British Designer for Industry Award. For three years running in the 1990s, he was named *GQ* magazine's Designer of the Year. In 1994 he was awarded a C.B.E. for services to fashion design and was knighted in 2000. Smith was the subject of the exhibition 'True Brit' at the Design Museum, London, subsequently shown in Japan at the Kobe Fashion Museum and the Mitsukoshi Museum of Art. For many years Paul Smith was also a fully-paid-up member of the Dennis the Menace club and still knows the secret handshake off by heart.

William Gibson

William Gibson is a world traveller, psycho-geographer, and keen military horologist. He lives in Vancouver, British Columbia, and holds an honorary degree of Doctor of Fine Arts from Parsons School of Design of the New School of Social Research.

Translators

'Paul Smith: A Most Benevolent Marvel' by William Gibson was translated into Japanese by Mizuhito Kanehara, into Italian by Massimo Birattari, into French by Pierre Girard and into German by Peter Robert.

Harold Smith

Harold Smith (1903–1998), Paul Smith's father, was a credit draper and amateur photographer. Co-founder of the Beeston Camera Club, he lived and worked in Nottingham, England.

Richard Williams

Richard Williams is the chief sports writer of *The Guardian*. He first met Paul Smith in Nottingham in 1966, when he would often stop by The Birdcage, the first shop Paul Smith worked in, to examine a new batch of button-down shirts or turtleneck sweaters on his way to covering fires, traffic accidents, funerals, court cases and golden wedding anniversaries for the local evening newspaper.

Jim Davies

Jim Davies is a writer and cultural commentator. His work has appeared in specialist design and advertising titles including *Eye, Print, IDEA* and *Ray Gun,* as well as *GQ, The Guardian, The Financial Times* and *The Sunday Times Magazine.* He is author of *The Book of Guinness Advertising,* plus the first chapters of several unfinished novels. He lives in Warwickshire with his wife and two young sons, where he listens to too much Al Green.

Hans-Ulrich Obrist

Since 1993 Hans-Ulrich Obrist has curated exhibitions for ARC Musée d'Art Moderne de la Ville de Paris and for the Museum in Progress, Vienna. He has also organised exhibitions by Christian Boltanski, Gerhard Richter and other artists, as well as group shows at the Hayward Gallery, London, the CAPC, Bordeaux, the Vienna Secession, Centro Belem, Lisbon, and the Sir John Soanes Museum, London. He is Editor-in-Chief of *Point d'Ironie,* published by agnès b, and has edited the writings of Gerhard Richter, Louise Bourgeois and Gilbert & George.

James Flint

James Flint's first novel *Habitus* won him the Amazon.co.uk 2000 Bursary Award; his second, *52 Ways to Magic America* – the story of a magician who starts an Internet company – will be published by Fourth Estate in January 2002. Between novels, he works as a contributing editor for *mute* magazine, www.metamute.com.

Professor Semir Zeki

Professor Semir Zeki is Professor of Neurobiology at the University of London (University College London) and co-head of the Wellcome Department of Cognitive Neurology. He is author of *Inner Vision,* an exploration of art and the brain (Oxford University Press) and co-author of *La Quête de l'Essentiel* (Archimbaud, Paris) with the late French painter, Balthus.

Paul Smith

Paul Smith, 27-year-old former window cleaner turned photographer, was born in Birmingham and moved to London eight years ago. He has been building his reputation as a photographer since 1999.

Jonathan Ive and Carter Multz

The expanded polystyrene (EPS) case for this book was designed by Jonathan Ive, with CAD by Carter Multz, in Cupertino, California, with additional CAD by Brian Neeson of Springvale EPS Ltd, Northern Ireland.

Aboud•Sodano

Aboud•Sodano is a compact design and photographic collaborative based in London, fronted by the founders who each share half its name. Alan Aboud and Sandro Sodano continue to enjoy the kind of loose, creative association they have had since they left St Martins School of Art in 1989. It's a kind of 'open' relationship, which allows them to do their own thing or even collaborate with others. But afterwards they tend to return to the fold, and still team up on a regular basis.

Scheufelen Premium Papers

Grateful thanks to Scheufelen Premium Papers UK for the supply of a range of Paralux and PhoeniXmotion papers for this book.

Tyvek® Brillion™

The Paul Smith comic book, *The Bunny,* was printed on Tyvek® Brillion™, an environmentally friendly material manufactured by DuPont®.

Expanded Polystyrene Packaging Group

The machine tool for the fabrication of the expanded polystyrene (EPS) case for this book was sponsored by the EPS Packaging Group, UK. This case was manufactured in Northern Ireland by Springvale EPS Ltd. EPS is an environmentally friendly, recyclable material.